Instructions to a Self:
A Diary of Becoming

Instructions to a Self:
A Diary of Becoming

jen lee

Jen Lee Productions
New York

Book design by Liz Kalloch.
Cover and author photos by Lisa Field.

For information contact Jen Lee Productions at www.jenleeproductions.com
ISBN-13: 978-0-9962384-1-0

Please
give us the right language
for whatever this is

Please
give us the gift
of good healing

–Anne Carmack
from *My Own Body Breathing*

Introduction

August 10, 2020

If you opened up my body you would find so many things unsaid, like residue built up over years. I imagine it like this photo a friend recently shared of a water pipe from her 100-year-old building. The cross-section showed no visible path left inside for actual water to flow.

Now I am trying to say the things more and more so the body of my body will not be full of build-up, but have space for breath and blood and music and flow, like a Hayao Miyazaki world inside me. Blowing grass and whimsical creatures who exist without self-consciousness or apology: Of course this is our universe, and we are alive in it.

Right here, right now I feel this spaciousness inside me. I do not hold things in like this—I don't want to use words like *ever* or *never*, but I have my eye on it. Now the holding in and not saying feel unnatural to me. I know inside I may have years and years of build-up, but wouldn't it be lovely to clear it all out, like Marie Kondo moving kindly from closet to closet with a sweet smile on her face?

There has not always been time or space or a feeling of safety in which to say things as I went, these last years. I felt like a cannonball being shot out of cannon after cannon, as if a person was walking down a row of them and lighting them one after another. Fuse. Fuse. Fuse. Fuse. Sometimes without even 24 hours between.

Now it feels like catching my breath, like noticing the unspoken things when they rise up and saying them. Maybe in the darkness on my bed with my teen as she wraps her arms around me.

Maybe I am saying too much, I tell her. I don't know where the lines are anymore.

Mom, she says, my lines are miles away from yours and you aren't likely to cross them even if you try.

This is what feels good. It might take some time to shake off my self-consciousness about the new Saying Things Way of Living, but I keep thinking of my friend's pipe, so stopped up with corrosion that water could no longer flow, and I know so clearly: Not that. Not that, for me or for us.

Not anymore.

April 2020

Wednesday, April 15, 2020

Day 34 at home.

I want to tell you about the little things. I want to tell you it's the little things that send me over the edge while I hold the big ones together. It's not finding a pen I like and the way I think I will tear the clothes off my body in despair for not having a good pen. The truth is, I will think, "I could kill myself," and then immediately edit out the thought. A person can't say that. It means something you don't really mean. And this will highlight how I am 40 something years old and still, this limited language for emotion that's hardly evolved past my 16 year old chorus of, "I hate my life," which actually meant something more like: I'm overwhelmed and expecting too much of myself. I don't have a life that leaves space for rest and it's exhausting me. I don't know what this boyfriend wants from me, but it's probably something sexual my devout teen self is not allowed to give.

It meant: I'm trying myself into the ground. And I'm lonely in here, inside this kaleidoscope of sensation and emotion. I'm missing the filter or the blinders or the numb button everyone else was born with, or the strategy book they acquired along the way.

It meant: Being good is stealing my life force and covering my path like a fog and what I really want is to feel home inside of me, no matter what the day holds. I want myself held steady in a place where I can breathe. I want to rest my head, I want to linger inside an embrace forever. I want to be connected but also independent in the good way, in the standing on my feet way, but I want my hands held, not empty. I want to walk into, step into, collapse into the day, the unknown and the night together. I want my face to let go of everything my cheek muscles are holding. They are so tired and overworked they dream of the grave. What happens if I let go. What will my face show, what truth will it tell. Will my skin slide right off my face and then will I get a new one?

A new face to face the day with to fall into love with to tell the truth with. A face that doesn't lie, not even for someone else, not even to be strong. A face that lets a heart run free across its field, unedited. Hello, day. I come just as I am and I don't have to be afraid of my anger or sadness and I don't have to pretend the life I was told to want is actually the life I do want. I can say with this face, "No thank you." I can walk away. I can cry about it and sleep until I can get up again and my new face and I will find the life I was meant to love.

Thursday, April 16, 2020

What if you thought of it as a returning, a rest, a replenishing or a refill? What if it was the refueling station of your dreams—time suspended and expectations lifted. What if you could extend your limbs long into the day, stretching like an animal after waking? The only choreography: a state of almost forgetfulness in its automatic invisible and interior origins.

What if you thought of it as no wrong steps taken up to this point, just the ones that brought you here, without judgment. What if there are only the steps you will take from here, outside right or wrong. Just the path now emerging. Just *a* way, not *the* way. Not just what you can see now and what you know now but something, somehow even deeper than those things and more inexplicable, like the animal stretch. Just your limbs, your muscles and skin and your heart aching to reach out and not hold artificially still and in place. What if those instincts were just as valid and true as their intellectualizing argumentative friends? What a world that would be. We would have to redefine what knowing looks like and what guise wisdom can arrive in and what the holiest of truths can be.

Ground down into a weariness that doesn't let you try for things you no longer desire. Ground into memories of being seen and heard and known and held with careful hands.

Ground into the animal part of you and its unique rhythms and hungers. When it wants sun give it sun, when it wants shady shelter lie in it. When it wants to feast on decadent dreams, weave them in long lingering fabrics. Dreams like a meal that can replenish our hungry places. Dreams like the lives we thought we'd have better hope for next time. Dreams like red meat, like a watering hole. Like a ballgown you could drape yourself in. And then maybe the dreaming becomes a map inside you that says when to migrate, when to hunt, when to droop lazy eyelids down to the ground of your cheeks. Maybe the dream would come to life with its own heartbeat and automatic breathing lungs and maybe it would dream you back to life.

Maybe the dream could dream you.

And could you let it? Could you surrender, without judgment or argument, or strategizing over whether it's really the best move? Could you feel the itch in your feet and step them?

Could you feel your deep abdomen, and all it is holding and let something deep within you go—pour out and spill as though out of a deep, wide bowl. Could you let it run like a river and rise like an ocean and fall back onto its surface and float?

What is the tide waiting to unleash?

Here is what I want you to know. Your body cannot contain it much longer. Your light and your life is calling. Soon it will be time to lift your head and stretch your animal stretch as if you have always done it. As if you always knew how.

Friday, April 17, 2020

First line from "Today When I Could Do Nothing" by Jane Hirshfield

Today when I could do nothing but make coffee and lift my head, I did this. I collected corduroy pants, newly folded on the shelf, and put them on with a sweatshirt stolen from one of my best friends. It felt like dressing myself in comfort and tenderness. I woke the children and it distracts from the ways I am trying to wake myself. "I am still sleeping," they sometimes cry, and this voice is in me, too.

I am still sleeping.

Don't wake me yet. Not into a new life of my own creating.

Don't wake me until I am done dreaming. Let the dreaming,
please, be my guide. How I have not left time for this before.
How I have woken too early maybe but certainly launched into
days structured by duty and light oh so light on desire.

Don't wake me until I am strong again. Over and over I think
of a chrysalis these days and feel myself inside of one, as maybe
we all are right now. And some days I am dissolving into soup
inside of it. And some days I feel myself taking a new shape. I try
not to be afraid of the way I might not recognize myself when
I emerge. Will I let myself do this deep becoming, this deep
unbecoming, this stillness that looks like a mummy from the
outside? Will I trust my own life?

I dream of air after a life on the ground. I dream of flight,
yes, but of wind and this magic called lift. I dream of gliding,
perching and diving. I dream of atmosphere and unseen forces
keeping me alight. I dream of hair down and wild. I dream of
unafraidness like a child wears it. I dream of gusts and swells and
gentle breezes. It's not floating—it's flight.

I dream of myself lifting my eyes my gaze my heartness to both
sun and moon in salute. In sacred offering.

But now, just now I dream of stillness. Please let it not end
before I'm ready to emerge. Something deep is happening in me,
something blue like the color not the mood. The collective calls
me but my answer today is not yet. My answer today is wait for
me.

I come. I come.

Saturday, April 18, 2020

What is it you want to remember? This soft cat curled into a circle of gray, like velvet. Certainly remember how bare this small potted tree looks. Yes, you left it out in the cold and so many leaves were sacrificed, but new leaves are coming like tiny stars shooting in slow motion from something tiny, low and barely visible. With time they will rise and spread and turn sunlight into life again. I feel you, I think now. So battered and bare, like you've been in a bad fight. But I remember how you come back and it helps me think maybe I will do the same.

I will remember this is the week I felt my own new places emerging, like their own tiny green stars. Not everyone can see them yet but it's enough for me to feel them and know they have come and are coming still.

I will not be this bare forever.

I will remember, I hope, how tired life has left me and how I learned how to rest. Like no one is waiting impatiently for my return. How to rest as if the whole world is asleep alongside me. It's taken so long to downshift into this gear that I wasn't sure I would get there. But I'm learning how to let the days be their own kind of medicine and my heart do its own kind of healing. It's like my body, which doesn't need to be told how to flush out a wound with blood and form a protective scab. Maybe a heart has its own automatic mending and my only role is to live an ordinary life as I pass through time, like a long tunnel. Time like a wide field shrouded in mist. Time like the sun and moon wrapping days around me like bandages. Like silk.

Let this be life now: my children and the way they inhabit a circle inside my arms. The dishes waiting to be made clean and the sheets ready to move to the dryer. This overcast rainy day light saying, No Heroics Just Now, Please. This soft light teaching me about Saturday, not as a concept but as a way of being. Saturday as a posture of surrender, as a stillness that holds me while I reach from low, tiny stars of new growth into something strong, nourished and self-sufficient again.

Saturday like a long, quiet sigh.

Evening (PM)

I am so weary right now, I might let myself say that I don't always know what comes next. But I do know what helps me feel alive. Finding my voice, hearing it and allowing it to be heard. The connection that comes after and how it obliterates the aloneness of my aloneness in a chorus of "Yes, for me, too." The relief and reminder—I really can trust myself to see things inside myself and then say them. Without trembling or regrets.

To find myself in the company of others is the sweetest kind of relief. Is there a way to make a job of this or a contribution out of this thing that makes me feel alive? What would it look like to get to mine for this, like gold or buried treasure and become skillful at the sharing? What if I am already there and simply not acknowledging it. What if I never really stopped? What if I have just rested while I could and mended as I went and held myself together like my patchwork quilt, always losing stitches here or there?

Maybe what is changing now is needing the outside world

a little less. Being uninterested in an audience or listener or recipient and catching myself first and foremost for myself. Having a relationship with myself that doesn't require any outside person to guide me here. There is just me coming home to myself.

Today I was longing for a certain landscape–mist, fog, maybe a lake surrounded by evergreens. What if the landscapes I could explore are inside of me? This is not a show on Netflix I need to find, it's a mood. This is the mood inside me today–deep mist, trees peeking through like sentinels and a source of water, of refreshment, of healing elements nearby. The more I find and map out my interior world, the less I miss and need others. I do not need a mirror to find myself. I just need my own hand on my own heart. I have missed this landscape, or I mistook it for something outside of me instead of something I carry within me. Oh water, I want to swim in you. Oh mist, I want you to obstruct the obvious pathway and lead me somewhere surprising. Oh evergreens, my color unchanging from season to season, my steady growth through time.

Moist, loose earth. My steadiness. My fertile soil and future.

I could drive through this landscape forever.

Monday, April 20, 2020

Here are a couple things I don't want to talk about. The way my body feels well and then unwell. The way a headache rolls in just as things were looking up. The way I have tantrums when I run out of pens (the good ones) or paper, as if I will lose my entire mind over these two precious supplies. I don't want to talk about how it's hard to feel close to friends when they inhabit other spaces. When they are looking "out there" for love or security and I am feeling so bound to finding them "in here" right now. I know I have all the moments—we all do.

I don't want to talk about love right now. I don't even like hearing songs about it. It feels like the latest religion I'm not sure if I still believe in or not.

I remember this feeling before. "Don't ask me where I've landed until I'm done unraveling." Maybe it's that moment. I don't want to talk about how it makes me feel ungenerous to turn away from people I care about when they choose another way or have a different feeling. How I think whatever I'm stepping into is fragile or must be protected. Other people and their ways are not a threat. I feel like a child to even have to say so.

What am I afraid of, really? Not having a net to catch me if the bottom falls out, if I make a mistake or don't see disaster coming from a mile away? What am I afraid of, really. Come on. Come on.

What. Am. I. Afraid. Of. Really. Being the main character in a tragic tale. Longing for something I cannot ever have. Feeling like other people won the lottery and I just played the game. I'm afraid of trying too hard or not hard enough. I'm afraid my body will obliterate my progress or crumple me to the ground. I am afraid there will not be enough coffee even though I was taught to be like the lily of the field and not worry about such things. I am afraid of who will be my god now and what is worthy of my faith. I worry I might not get another chance.

What if I could believe in happy endings, but not the kind we were sold. The new kind, full of surprises. Happy endings about the "in here" that's been here all along. In this posture is there anything to fear, really, or simply trust in our resilience? Trust in mine. I am listening and working and waiting but maybe the finish line is always this spot where we are now standing.

Tuesday, April 21, 2020

This isn't where the poem begins, or the song. Under these covers, my head propped up by this wall. This is just the rhythm of a body. This ache in my head that comes on cue like the timpani, waiting for their big moment after the crescendo.

These are the days I survive, with a tenderness in my cheekbones and an ache deep in my belly. I don't feel poetic in this state, or animated. I do not feel like dancing. Only this deep stillness until it passes like rain clouds on a day with no wind.

I will take what the stillness holds. Sometimes a glimpse behind a curtain, other times maybe a simple letting go of dishes and surfaces. Letting someone else step into my place. Maybe there will not be words today, but my mind, she is still in there.

Still simmering aromatic brews in a variety of pots.

Today there is some kind of hallelujah, and maybe this is where the song begins: in our frailty and our surrender. Oh body, I hear you. I will lay down while the tide turns. I will do what I can and relinquish the rest.

It is the song of Beyond Myself, or its opposite—Within Myself, and no more. Maybe the song begins in my acceptance, which feels like turning my face upward into a downpour. It feels like the kind of rain that washes the clothes right off of you, until you are reduced to only yourself. No more, no less, nothing added, clutched, carried or tried. Just head back, face up surrender. Arms dropped and palms loose. There is nothing to reach for. There is only the rain and the way it teaches you your contours and shape.

Maybe this is the song.

Maybe the something in my belly is one hundred percent physical. Maybe it is something deep and yearning, trying to spill out. Maybe it is the hearth fire that warms me or the locomotive coal fire powering me. Maybe this is simply the rest required to roll the way I roll. I try not to be afraid the world won't wait for me or hold me in the meantime.

I try to love these cheeks even in their aching. Thank you bed and sheets and sunlight through the window. Thank you blooms out the window and sirens finally slowing. Thank you day leading to the next one. Thank you heart on a body-built altar. Thank you faith in the turning tides—even the ones inside us.

Thank you slowing down and waiting and invisible stitches in quiet places. Thank you womb, and moon, and night.

Thursday, April 23, 2020

What if I were to tell you that we are sometimes happy here,
tucked into this apartment like small children under heavy quilts
just before snowfall? What if I were to tell you that even in
the midst of difficulty and uncertainty we are finding our own
softness, and joy and light? The way we can be better if we let
what we were holding fall gently and quietly apart.

What if I told you the kitten likes to get close when I'm
writing. Nose into my coffee cup, corner of my notebook in his
teeth before flying off the desk and continuing his search.

I am reminded sometimes of the hard parts ahead, of the things
that feel like bad news to break. I'm sure there will be more
moments of fear or loneliness but these days it feels more like
lightness. Is this the magic of surrender, or a mercy embedded
in acceptance? Something about allowing things to be just as
they are without judgment or blame. It lets us be something else
besides angry or wronged. We get to be witnesses, truth-tellers.

We get to be brave. We get to be kind.

I'm grateful for having told one long story, even though it
was so sad I took to my bed for days. I'm grateful for what it
showed me. The things I've lived without and the ways I've tried
patching together replacements. How it might be possible to have
something more whole.

How I might become something more whole.

The spring flowers are everywhere. In the trees and on the
ground. I can't stop admiring them, photographing them, like
someone smitten with a new love. How I want to take in beauty—
actually ingest it somehow to carry with me. Could it be spring

inside me, always? At least in one small room at the end of the hall where we keep the door closed to preserve the sweet smell.

Could it be spring inside me always. Even though it is winter and nightfall and fallow fields that make the blooms so cherished. There are those times but it's important to let myself have this one.

Hope. Unhurriedness. Loving the children and baking the celebratory cake with cream cheese frosting for one of my beloved kids.

How I love them.

If there were only four words in the world I could keep, it might be those.

Take this lily pad of peace. Close your eyes and let something in you stitch back together and heal. There is the future, yes I smell it, too. But really today there is only today. Release forms and differential equations and the end of a long, life-saving journey.

Just taste it. Take bite after bite.

And let it be sweet.

Friday, April 24, 2020

Here's what I want you to know. How grateful I am that when she's weeping she wants to be in my arms. That she lets me hold her. I feel an old script rising up inside me—a chasten for watching stories that hurt her. But this is not useful to me anymore. I will not make her feel wrong for wanting to face things directly and know them. I will not make her wrong for letting things break her heart.

Sorrow is so often correct. And too often, horror. Outrage. Heartache of the highest measure and deepest depths. I understand now my job is not to protect her from pain but to embrace her in it and stay close beside as she walks through it. As sometimes her strong face and body give way to it. Yes. This is how we are. If some things do not make us weep we are not paying attention.

Here is what I want you to know. I have some hard truths of my own to deliver and I know they will break their hearts. I want to remember how it felt today, to not try and take it away from her or rush her through it. But just holding. Sitting close. Kissing and wiping tears.

How bad news or hard things have moved through my own body before. Sometimes sending me into shock for days. But the body digests things, and maybe the heart does too. We taste bitterness and toughness between our teeth. But on and on we chew until we can somehow swallow.

Today a wise woman talked of failure and how it's necessary and I do want to live a brave life that isn't afraid to step into unknown futures, or try for things. I want the kids to live this way, too—unafraid of missteps or experiments and whatever may come.

I want us all to learn we can pick up and begin again, as new versions of ourselves. Maybe a bit battered but with knowledge and wisdom newly, maybe even painfully, planted inside us. I am trying to imagine a work future for myself and I am trying to trust something is waiting there for me. Do I need to dream it into being? Or say yes to it or pray for or wait for it?

I do not know.

What I do know is I work better when I am not afraid. I know I have some reason to have hope. I know there are options I do not know about and sometimes the missing ingredient is time. For now I rest. I get organized. And I wait.

Listen. Pray. Keep banging down the walls inside me that insist on winning a game whose rules I no longer subscribe to. I wait. At least for today. I hold my kid and take notes on this for another day.

But I don't have to live that one just yet.

Saturday, April 25, 2020

Why You Should Pick Me

1. I'll look dead into your eyes, then all the way down to your heart.
2. I like the feeling of soft things.
3. I fall in love over and over again. With the cherry blossoms, every time they bloom. With winter branches and summer waves.
4. I am getting a new face. One that tells the truth in all its hardness. One that pours out affection in all its softness.
5. I feel like coming home.
6. I know how to hold a head against my chest.

7. I do not know what I will do for someone I love but I think there will be something good to eat or drink.
8. I will let myself be taken care of.
9. I remember the important things, like the way your eyes look when you smile.
10. I listen to jazz, nostalgic tunes that make life feel like a movie.
11. Linus the kitty can attest I give good belly rubs.
12. Something inside me is tender and
13. something inside me is fire.
14. I almost know how not to burn wild.
15. The way my hand loves another hand, as though it were something sacred. Something all on its own alive.
16. Wild hair don't care.
17. I am learning to be with all the parts of life, even the hard ones.
18. I'm braver than I've ever been before.
19. I lay on the ground and feel the earth holding me, so I'll know how to hold myself and how to be held.
20. I can be right here,
21. and I can go anywhere.
22. I am strong now.
23. But I will let you do your side of the thing.
24. I will sit next to you in the dark and run alongside you, laughing, into the light.

Sunday, April 26, 2020

If you really knew me, you'd know how to read my face or hear the truth in my voice. You would know I don't always like to say it straight out. But I am learning.

If you really knew me, you'd know how hard I work and how I don't give up easily. You would feel the future in the squeeze of my hand in yours.

This isn't a poem for rainy days.
For gloomy skies or the bottom falling out.
This isn't a poem for yesterday's flowers, or last year's hope.
This poem is for looking straight at the things
you've danced around, wrestled with, argued and railed against.
This poem is for looking at the truth. Even if it makes you
pull the blanket over your face and weep.
Even if you storm out of the room
as if you could outrun bad news
and slam a door in its face.
As if it wouldn't follow.
As if it hasn't always been among us somehow,
like a pandemic spreading while some vacation in remote places
and are just now hearing the news.
The truth is always there, this poem tells you.
Whether you name it or not.
Whether you let your lips shape it.
Whether you hold it out of sight or let it full-on
break your heart.

How beautiful, the breaking, this poem will say.
How full of hope those dreams, how earnest was your longing.
How tireless your efforts and how devastating this surrender.
This final truth-telling that has been felt
but not acknowledged.
There is not the kind of love here one needs.
There are other kinds, perhaps, that will carry
other kinds of days.
But not a love to carry this one.
This day must be laid to rest,
and so many you imagined to come after,
a domino run never toppled.

This poem will tell you how beautiful is the beginning.
How brave it is to face, and step into.
All the knowing and not knowing
swimming together like an oil spill at sea.
How beautiful is the beginning.
How lucky, the one who can hear a new song, and play it.
How tender but free we will someday be.
Even today, more together in the knowing
than we were yesterday.

This poem won't put broken things back together.
It won't tuck you in, or hold you tight.
But your arms are stronger now,
your face lifts up in the face of hard things,
when it used to duck.
Or turn away.

This poem will remind you,
How beautiful the breaking.
How beautiful the beginning.
And how brave the facing, the holding and the uplifting.
Forever and ever, amen.

Monday, April 27, 2020

This is the part I don't want to tell you. That yesterday I had
chocolate cake with every meal, but today it is difficult to taste, to
chew and to swallow. I don't want to admit how tired I am, how
something wants to sleep itself off of me—something that can't
work itself out any other way or be rushed.

I don't want to talk about the times when my optimism wanes,
when I feel at a work-related crossroads. How I forget who I am
or grow uncertain of what form to take.

This is the part I don't want to tell you—how fleeting and
seldom love sometimes feels, how a certain romantic love seems
something I might need to live without, like a nun.

But that is not what Francisco says. I don't want to tell you the
part where a Spanish-born psychic is one of my guiding lights.
How he gives words I was missing and is full of reassurances
and pictures. I feel the least afraid when I walk away from his
Greenwich Village front door.

Today I will spend time with the words of Francisco. Today I
will rest and let something sleep out of me. Something like shock

or disappointment or uncertainty. Or all three. When I am rested it's easier to be in action. The motions come decisively, with little effort. There's fluidity and flow. I can tend this flame with good rest when I need it. The work pulls me forward and through, yes, but that doesn't always mean motion. Sometimes it can mean Masterclass in bed and soft light through the window and aftershocks moving through my arms and the muscles in my face.

This is the part I don't want to tell you–that I don't want to get stuck in the resting, nor do I crave a spotlight. Let me please find a way into something between.

What is making you tired?

Being unloved and living each day inside love's absence. The way it stretches across the sofa and plays its video games so loudly. The way it doesn't know which clothes are mine and puts them in my kids' piles. The way it doesn't care to hear about my day or know how to react to big news or small.

It is exhausting to live in love's absence. My face droops and my head knows how to look away now, how to do-si-do past each other in the hallway. The way it highlights all the places love could live here, if its heart were still beating.

If love were here it would spread a blanket on the roof, it would rub feet through thick wool socks and watch the light slowly say goodbye to the day. Love would reach out to touch one's cheek. It would offer a comforting embrace. Love might say, Can I make your coffee? Love might draw a bath. It might keep vigil until you fall asleep and murmur, Good Morning, when you wake.

Love might really love the dress with red polka dots you got last year for your birthday but couldn't wear because of the mosquitoes. Love might dream of seeing you in it, smiling in red lipstick. Love might long for your summer clothes, and for walking beside the way you gently sway in those heels. Love might plan picnic dinners, even if they were only on the roof this year. Love might love your books and jewelry pieces and treasures. It would want to live inside your world with you, under your sheets and tangled in your windblown hair.

PM

Often in the mornings, particularly on a Monday morning, I spend a good amount of time puttering. I gather up trash and recycling. We're at the point now of using cereal bag liners as trash bags. I water the plants because their leaves are curling or drying up. I decide to let the small pot go. The second plant has now died in it. I rearrange my desk drawer, pulling out the broken reading glasses. They are my best pair. My first pair. The ones I picked out with my mother in a bookstore called The Tattered Cover.

"I've repaired them once before," I tell her. "It's time to let them go."

"It's a practice for me now," I go on. "Letting go of broken things."

"I've noticed," she says. We aren't talking about bookstore readers now but this is how it comes out of me—not just in the big things but in the little ones, too.

"It's depressing to keep looking at them," I say, and drop the pieces into a cereal box-liner bag.

Tuesday, April 28, 2020

You don't have to be a hero. Just do the day in front of you. Hot coffee, lukewarm peppermint tea. The way we didn't sleep well so we're going gently. How tired I was yesterday, but this morning resumés went flying out before 9am. Linus stretched out and snoozing, a high school video on pause. The way today you can reach out to the future with a little faith and no desperation.

No heroics just now. Try a little realism, and then a walk in the sunshine. A class you could take if your mind can make space for it. A week off from your usual responsibilities. Time for taxes and the form you didn't know you needed.

So often life is like this: you make the spreadsheet and keep the receipts, and yet. There is still the form you didn't see coming, and it's already late.

You don't have to be a hero. Maybe just make them something to eat. Allow their grief to come in unexpected ways, like a nap before lunch. Keep the clothes washed.

Read the postings.

Hit submit.

Wait for the story to come back.

Rest, dear one. You can rest, too.

I always thought I could hold it together and see the future coming, but we see when it's time and not a minute sooner. We ask the future to meet us, right here, with a little more confidence than we had last year.

Let the future that wants me turn its head when I cross its path. Let it do a double take. Let it be surprised when I'm a little like what it was searching for, but better.

Let me have a home in the world, in this city, in the fabric of things. Let me be a home that things are born in, home to a light that radiates and illuminates.

I guess today I feel like prayer. Prayer and trust because I'm thankfully too weary to worry. But I can drizzle blue ink across this wide page. I can drip and dance the words. I can find the ones you're missing or never imagined you'd need.

This pen will be my good company for now, this heart my good friend. These children, my comfort and this sun the never-ending light on my life.

The world is ready, if I will keep telling it I'm here, I'm here, I'm here.

You don't have to be a hero today.

Just steady on. Light on your feet and soft-faced. Ready to nourish, to play. And be fed.

Hallelujah. Head bowed. Heart open.

Wednesday, April 29, 2020

25 Things

1. I'm obsessed with the Great American Songbook and lately Louie and Ella are really getting me through.
2. Jazz reminds me of my grandfather, and the way he and my grandmother looked dancing.
3. I'm pulling out the soft things lately, like black velvet pants. I like to describe my favorite clothing style as "wearable

blankets." I prefer garments that could double as pajamas.

4. But I've been trying to build a new wardrobe for going out. Blouses with structure, boots with heels.

5. I bought myself a new lipstick from Whole Foods for my new year. Look out, 2020. These lips are comin' for you.

6. My friends are my life lines.

7. I love hard, which I guess translates to losing big when it's gone.

8. I travel through the world with an arm around each of my children, invisibly if not literally. This is my heart posture.

9. I don't know when to quit, but I am learning. I've never liked feeling I'm giving up.

10. But I'm learning I can choose again.

11. Blue blankets forever.

12. Making spaces beautiful doesn't come naturally to me, but I've tried to learn because beauty is so nice to live inside of.

13. I wish we could have flowers on the table, all the time.

14. I've loved a good bass singer ever since I was a child.

15. Road trips with people I love are one of life's great joys.

16. Second only to train travel. Oh to watch the world go by out big windows, rackety rhythm and just the right speed for bringing one's heart along in real time.

17. I'm still working out all the ways I feel inextricably linked to my roots, even as I forge a new path.

18. Sisters and brothers forever.

19. Nature refuels me. I can bathe in moon and starlight or be completely powered by sunlight.

20. I never feel like I do with a camera in my hands. Maybe at my mother's piano. Maybe.

21. I can't stop thinking in movies, in stories, even if I try.
22. I'm learning a new kind of faith. I don't have good words for it just yet.
23. I want to be seen, and I want to be hidden. I'm learning to lean into the former.
24. And I'm learning how to rest.
25. There's nothing like a good song.

Thursday, April 30, 2020

I caught myself thinking about drowsiness and how it's hard to shake off. How it's hard to sleep so many times I wish I could. But today I walked across Prospect Park in the rain and sleep should come easily tonight.

I caught myself thinking about people who are far away, and someone I miss terribly. Wondering when that will back off and also if there's a better place for my attention to go.

Sometimes I think about a numbness in my body and wondering if I should be trying harder to coax it awake. Essential oils rubbed into my feet or something like trying to bring back an appetite with especially yummy food.

Maybe it's better to wait it out and let it come back in its own time. If some part of me is a balloon drifting away I wonder if it should be tied to my wrist so it doesn't drift too far.

I caught myself thinking about the potted tree in my window. It lost so many leaves recently when I tried transitioning it to the fire escape before it was done getting too cold.

It looked barren and half-dead at first. Then miniature stems and leaves started appearing and emerging.

It looks so proud now, with one tiny star of new leaves left. I want to photograph it so I don't forget how quickly we can grow back. It feels slow during the day, yes, and invisible.

But the stacking of days works a slow and invisible kind of miracle. You look over and just like that: it's back.

I caught myself thinking about the future and how I can hold it lightly. How I don't want to miss an opportunity to rest and refuel after all this time of caffeinating my way through days and weeks and months and years.

Holding steady feels like this. It feels like acceptance and patience. It feels like actions when I can and a soft bed when I can't lift my arms any longer.

What will someday be like? I have no idea but I am grateful to be alive in this day, with nowhere in particular to go besides the kitchen, crowded with yesterday's dirty dishes. I'll need a happier song to wash them.

This one makes me want to lie down and stay there for seven years.

Today there was also a new notebook, but my daughter thinks I should finish this one first so it will be less hodge podge.

I want to write about the leaky roof and broken turntables but every day I forget.

May 2020

Friday, May 1, 2020

I remember this feeling in my arms before, when I was pregnant with Amelia. By 8pm I couldn't hold my arms up enough to knit, and for at least a year I set my knitting needles down. It's that sensation again. And I know I walked over an hour yesterday but my arms feel as if I had walked on them and not my legs.

It makes me wonder: What am I gestating now? What is happening inside to make my cells feel this stretched thin or overwhelmed?

It feels more like that time than like the return from Sweden, which left me disembodied and numb for weeks. Terrible bouts of vertigo would descend, making me reach for nearby furniture, countertops or walls to steady myself.

That was more a lack of feeling, which I did wake up with the other day. It's hard to even hold a pen sometimes because I can't feel my hands well.

If it's like that time, it's probably shock.

Shock. Grief. Gestating.

I'm birthing something new. A new future, a new life, a new version of myself.

It is big work. It's understandable why I might need quiet minutes under a heavy blanket with my arms at my side. Hold me, they say. There isn't a person here to hold them but there is this blanket, and I can hold them still.

I watch easy movies and wish sleep would come but small sporadic currents shoot down my legs. Keeping me restless and awake.

I don't know what I'm brewing exactly. But I'm interested in healing and not just getting through. I am holding myself back from overwork, even though some—quite a bit—of work calls today. I know some things can be slept off, that the body can heal itself, even from sorrow. That really letting myself experience the end of this road is the best bet on finding the start of the next one.

I want to rest in a way that isn't giving up or wasting time. Is such a thing even possible? What if nothing is ever wasted? What if I emerge from this in whatever state I do? Strong isn't necessarily winning and tender isn't weak.

But how I do long to find a strength or steadiness or deep foundation inside myself. My spirit card this month is about dharma and I'm trying not to get too caught up in my head about it. Whatever rises from this great weariness I will allow. Perhaps this is enough. Perhaps it is everything.

Saturday, May 2, 2020

Who knew that I would someday take a roof leak in stride, watch water raining down my bedroom wall as if it were the least of my problems? I guess it is. But more than that: I know something new. I know leaks happen. Walls can be cut out and rebuilt. Painted over. Soggy wood floors can be dried out. It's just temporary and someone will help fix it.

It's just a contrast from the first time it happened. How I panicked, how I felt such deep regret about repairing it without

confirming the leak had already been fixed. How peculiar that
the previous tenants lived with it so long. Maybe it was blocked
by furniture in the bedroom and rusty paint cans in the coat
closet.

Isn't it how we are so often?

Living with leaks eroding our walls and never even knowing.

I can tell it's been a lot of isolation when Mr. Oliver's son,
Jamal, who used to live in the bedroom I'm in now, came to pick
up his mother's stimulus check yesterday and I got teary from
that little human exchange. It's one thing I loved about living
in the city before the pandemic—so many small and unplanned
interactions like this could live inside a day.

Get down to it. The way you are being unraveled, trying to
find the deepest of the deep and the core of your core. Finding
the new form for the next season, even though we don't know
when that will be. Or what it will look like. Something about
the dissembling feels important—in part for the inner inventory:
What are my skills, gifts, abilities and capacities? But also for
the flexibility and fluidity of it. Look: I could be so many things
next.

What I long for is community and I'm wondering what form
this might take before the end, by which I mean a full return to
togetherness. Some interim season lies between here and there.

Get down to it. To my longing for love, for companionship.
My shaky belief in these things—where to find them, how they
sometimes don't last when you want them to, or linger when you
don't.

We are all falling into nostalgia. In my best moments I look for
the shape of my longings inside it.

But most of all today: a splitting headache I can hardly think through. A knowing I'll need to get back to work soon. Today, actually.

Hoping it will return me to a part of myself I'm fading without, like the color draining from my skin. Please some relief from the headaches, soon and very soon.

Sunday, May 3, 2020

10 Things Bringing Me Joy

1. The downstairs neighbors' apartment, abandoned for the pandemic, and my occasional escape. I go down every four days or so to water the plants. But it's also there if I need to simply "water the plants". The apartment is gorgeous— immaculately styled as if for sale, impeccable as a magazine. I step into this world to keep life alive in it. Tiny plants that droop easily and want their leaves misted, and bigger things like a fig tree that need hefting into the tub. There are Alexas in at least two rooms. Is anyone watching, I wonder. Is anyone listening? Mostly I just take long, deep breaths as if the oxygen is better inside their walls than in ours.

2. Having my children curled up beside me in bed. For a mid-morning nap or an early-morning BBC mystery. Sometimes, especially on the weekend, for a sleepover. We like each other close right now. We like Linus curled up with us, in

a circle with his small paws covering his eyes, or burrowed into a cave made of sheets and blankets.

3. The way light fills my room on a clear sunny day. Gentle and soft in the morning, growing to a crescendo late in the afternoon. I like that I can lie in bed and let it fall on me.

4. Soft clothes and elastic waists. The new items I bought before the pandemic and how they help me picture my future professional self. Lucy's leggings and the way they are growing short. Every soft and cozy piece of lounge wear we own. Bless the pajama pants.

5. My dear and beloved friends. The way they remember me, reach out and reach back. The way they keep me company.

6. Every blanket. The blue blanket with white tassels my parents and sisters went in together for my birthday when it was the only thing I wanted. The weighted one my parents gave us ago that is good for trauma. The gold plush ones they sent the year before that one. It's an easy theme to notice—the way we send a long-distance and everyday embrace.

7. Songs that have just the right beat. A cleaver lyric. A percussion that urges my feet forward and a swelling melody that lifts my head. Dancing isn't always easy to reach, but I can feel the Keep Going most of the time. Bam-bam-clap-clap-strum-strum-strum.

8. Writers that say the thing I didn't know how to say so I know I'm not the only one—they know this, too. Saints, all.

9. The way the light lands on my plant leaves. Like a spotlight drawing my attention: This is a live thing, just as you are living. This is a growing, healing thing whose past injuries

are scarcely visible. It reaches up to the sky, it defies gravity, it spreads wide and unapologetic to drink up the sun, gentle, soft or bright.

10. My self, this brave heart and fragile body. This love in me, the determination to find a way. This willingness to listen and to, in some kind of time, let go. We don't get new beginnings without allowing ourselves endings. A hard truth, but today I'm sitting with it. Palms open, head supported, belly soft.

Monday, May 4, 2020

Things to Do in a Pandemic

Make playlists. Listen to a song called Persephone again and again, but not so loudly you can't hear yourself think. Make your bed as soon as you get up, but climb right back under the covers again after breakfast with her beside you. Tackle things you are and are not looking forward to with company beside you. Your pen moves across a wide page and she reads about something called "desalination" and solves quadratic equations.

Forget about your eyebrows for days. Maybe weeks. Let the clean laundry linger on the dining table, today pushed aside to the far wall in a bid for space. Group games pull you now more than formal chairs, but that could change when your hormones swing around again. Just yesterday you felt well enough to clean the kitchen, and you did. Windexing the light fixtures is a particular state of wellness. Or a stage of isolation—it's hard to say anymore.

Throw open the windows and pretend it's the same thing as going outside. Lavish in the way outside can blow in, refreshing the smell and energy of a space. It's the rare window before the pollen turns brutal. Maybe today we will aspire to the magical cross breeze, where something blows in, blows out and through.

Pray without knowing it: Make us new.

Put off the market another day. Hang curtains from your last life. Some of them handed down from a life even before that one. Wake up the next morning and love the softness and rose-colored hue of their filtered light.

What a gentle awakening.

Wear the yoga pants again, why not? Keep the paths flowing, and the good hair days.

Take the supplements and feel hopeful about feeling better some day soon—more balanced, more well. How will the feeling better future feel? Will our complexions shine? Already we are not doing too badly.

I feel long days and brighter light carrying me. Try not to worry about next winter. It is like a planet you have not visited: Who can really imagine it? Instead make this apartment—your rocketship into whatever the future holds—your home. You are a space traveler now, any journey or adventure ahead will be lived just like this day. Moment by moment. Hour by hour. Sheets pulled up and down, light moving across the wall in a dance of shadow and spotlight.

Your heart beating as it is now. Your head held up, propped up or resting through so many moments that don't require your strenuous effort or strain. In sheltering, finally learning a rhythm more suitable for living.

Tuesday, May 5, 2020

I remember the curve at the back of your neck.

I remember the night sky in Central Park.

I remember those old floor tiles, little black and white hexagons on a restaurant bathroom floor.

I remember the textured wood tables of Le Pain. How they have held my elbows for rest and planning and tears.

I remember neighbors in fancy dress and elaborate hats dancing at the Prospect Park Soiree.

I remember hands. Seeing them and reaching for and holding them.

I remember aviator sunglasses and sun in my eyes and my father behind the wheel after making us laugh with rainbow wigs.

I remember missing friends and longing to see them again. It feels far away now, even the missing. Like an echo.

I remember the heat of summer and Flatbush in the hot sun.

I remember GiamPaolo filling the courtyard with beautiful things, like our own Italian piazza.

I remember how tight and short Otis' coat is, and how his tail wagged so hard it could bruise.

I remember *Murder She Wrote* with Annie and pints with friends— the ice cream kind and the beer kind.

I remember how content and happy I felt with Tabitha that last night out at the bar. How even then we were nervous and washing our hands rigorously. How I knew it was my last night out.

I remember the way my mother smells when I hug her. The feeling of her skin.

Dad's pancakes. In shapes and first initials of everyone's names.

The way my grandmother's eyes look when she laughs so hard she cries.

I remember the sun rising and setting behind an evergreen skyline in a Francestown field.

My aunt and the way she holds me.

I remember feeling suspended between continents but also celestial road maps or life timelines and finding my way back on a park bench overlooking the Manhattan skyline.

I remember feeling nervous. I remember excitement. My skin can almost remember that kind of touch.

I remember muffins from Colson Patisserie warmed with blueberries and served on a wooden platter.

I remember learning a new world. Again and again.

I remember the 4th of July fireworks. On my roof. On Bill and Launa's.

The New Year's Eve fireworks I watched alone in Grand Army Plaza. The perfect beginning for this strange new year.

I remember feeling alone and together there. Now the reverse, somehow. Together, alone.

PM

Today feels like folk music and a breeze coming through the window. Sore from walking, tender from sitting. What shape can I be in?

Today feels like my mother's soothing voice and Bella's oil on my face.

Today feels like black bean soup for dinner with homemade tortilla chips, and Good Omens on the couch.

Today feels like feeling my heart, like afternoon decaf and a second round of energy. The table back in place and towels washed.

Today feels like watching and wanting. Listening and working. So many days do.

Today feels like wanting my own words more than someone else's. Like setting down a strange record of a surreal time.

Today feels like my people are safe today and trying not to worry about tomorrow.

Tonight feels like I hope bedtime is soon, despite the decaf. It feels like the day, long and light and how can it already be time for dinner.

Tonight feels like rubbing my eyes and dirty dishes waiting and how I love the sound of her laugh.

Tonight feels like we don't need the fans today but a blanket would be nice.

Tonight feels like the only time and the only place, as we are relieved of imagining a future or dwelling too long inside it.

For now is the waiting, and the living and the hoping for more days after this one.

Wednesday, May 6, 2020

"We already love you." — *Laurie Wagner*

Instructions You Missed Along the Way

A pamphlet on the benefits of saying the things you're afraid to say out loud, complete with diagrams of one's esophagus blocked and clenched before, open and released after.

A data graph detailing how you are not yet where you will someday be. It will have numerous versions tracking important variables like patience and calm in the presence of volatility. Those will increase while things like upset over having dishes to wash will decrease.

A how-to video on how to preserve love through pain. The one that tells how to catch yourself mid-wounding and correct course before repeating again and again. A special feature outlines how to offer a good apology, one that doesn't stop short or hold back but goes all the way.

A road map showing all the many routes to purpose. All the places you could find yourself because you carry yourself to them.

The GPS that gives clear direction on when to stay and when to leave. In a thick fog, you deliberate whether to trust it but decide you have no other choice.

A master-level college course on how to leave gracefully. Without storming out the way your wounded heart often wants too—not in anger so much as that other thing. You saw it enacted once while babysitting, when the two-year-old cried, beside himself, throwing his body through the house room by room, eyes squeezed shut in anguish as you steered him away from coffee table corners.

The bedtime prayer that ushers you into carefree slumber every time.

A blueprint for hearts. A script for the tour. "Here is where I keep my dreams—closer to the path than my regrets. Every pebble under our feet hand painted with an intention or longing in a sea of purples, greens, and blues."

A weather guide for how to dress in every season. When to opt for softness and when it's time for structure. It doubles as a fashion guide. How to Wrap Yourself (or Shed Layers) for Every Mood.

An investor's guide whose only currency is connection.

A flashlight called What to Do Next that only illuminates a small half-circle in front of where your feet now stand.

The embroidered pillow that says, "We Already Love You".

Thursday, May 7, 2020

You can't have it all, but you can see and feel and appreciate what's yours for now. Time for a nap here before you, like a precious thing. How many times have you pushed through, made more coffee, trying to catch a second wind? How many times you thought the sunshine demanded you make time for leaving.

But now, when there are not movie theaters or coffees on Jess' sofa or salads at Maggie's. There is this: time for a nap. Your eyelids are already longing for it.

You can't have it all but you could take good care of all you do. Hearts, and trust, and friendship. This home that holds you. You know what it is to sleep on an air mattress for a month. This bed itself is a miracle of luxury and comfort.

You can't have it all, but hopefully the exchange will work in the end. Maybe instead of til death do we part there is a certain kind of freedom and agency to be as you are. You can't have it all but maybe some things are better than having. Becoming, for one thing. Also: unbecoming. Healing. Rebirth and salvation, if those are still words you carry.

Most of all, I know the way my heavy blanket feels on top of me, and the rocking melody of this song in my ears. I tuck myself in like a toddler hoping for good dreams.

Most of all, there is time, at least while we are still alive in it. Time that I have been racing or outrunning. But now it's something else. Something endless like a carton of milk that never runs out. Now time reworks me the way my cousin Scott said his year in Italy did. How I wanted that time transformation—to feel its breadth and spaciousness. Maybe I am feeling this now.

Most of all there are coverings for every weather. Three varieties of cocoa for an unusual snow coming this weekend. Winter, summer, holiday or school—we no longer have the knowing or the location for where we are in the rhythm.

But we have mugs. Three types of cocoa and spoons to stir them. We have a sunny day I'm passing on to rest instead. I have this Work in Progress shirt from Mindy and I'm wearing it now. I still have some of the things that make me beautiful even as I shed some that made me sharp, clumsy or rigid.

There is a small pillow in a satin pillowcase from my grandmother because it's good for curly hair. I have Linus sleeping beside me and I will be right behind him.

PM

I don't watch shows like I used to, and reading isn't always correct either.

More than anything I want my own words and my voice. More than anything I want to demolish the censor screens and walls I've built.

Just let it out, he said, the wall building up at super hero-speed in my eyes while he watched in dismay.

Just let it out now. How you want to live somewhere beyond approval or what other people think. How you could leave disappointing people in the gutter and carry something else instead. How there's something beyond striving you're looking for. Will you find it now, in a pandemic, in this bed that is happy to hold you for hours and days and years. Maybe you'll dismantle the fear of falling behind, and how it's maybe an imaginary thing and not an actual avalanche chasing you. Maybe you will learn the flavor of enough and lose your taste for striving. Maybe, finally learning to rest and making a home in its pleasure.

Friday, May 8, 2020

PM

I don't like to admit it, but I really love to win the game. Any game, really. School? Straight A's. Bank teller? Balancing to the penny. My high school self driving herself for some reason I can't remember. Maybe it was winning the game. Saving souls in the church, or recruiting new beauty consultants onto my direct selling team.

I wanted to win the follow our dreams to New York City game. The better life abroad game. The till death do we part game. The happy children game, the getting better game, the holding in the tears and stiff upper lip game. The stoicism of ancestors game. The golden child game.

How silly they feel now. I literally had to pause the pen for a gigantic yawn. This is the reaction I have to these things now.

Yawn. Yawn so big, tears stream out of the corners of my eyes.

Winning the games. I guess it got me somewhere but it couldn't take me all the way.

I guess now I'm learning the value of folding. Of leaving the games I want to leave. That simply, and the end.

I still catch myself wanting to frame this as a new, more self-developed kind of winning, a secret super win. It will take more time to dismantle this, perhaps, and leave my grid of winning and losing behind.

Even today, all day, I've been stuck on a gaming metaphor but now I guess the focus is on learning not to freak out when I'm dealt a difficult or painful hand. Now I'm learning to hold it with a soft expression around my eyes, my lips untensed. I shrug my shoulders up and down again a few times to keep loose on the outside and on the inside.

Now I just want to play well. Given these cards, what's the best I can do? Can I stay calm, even if it means folding. Can I stay gentle with myself. Can acceptance be my friend as I pull each card. Can I surrender to the elements of chance outside my control?

That's really the main thing. I've been heavy on control, trying to win even the clean kitchen game. But if I let go of winning I can reach the part of myself that's just grateful to play. The part that's learned that cards come and go and these will turn into others but no day is without risk, without the vulnerability it is to be alive in this world. The plumber and super will come and fix the toilet and snake the pipes. I will be grateful but also grossed out and also hoping a dangerous virus isn't transmitted. All the moments, all the feelings, are what makes it life. Not that white knuckled grip or strategizing, pretzel-making mind.

Saturday, May 9, 2020

Inspired by Laurie Wagner's "Rough Draft"

Let this be the year of giving up. Of letting things drop or fall apart. Letting the sky fall. Let this be the year of Too Tired to Pretend. Let this be the year of wanting what I want without apology.

It can also be the year of surrender. Waving the white flag.
Putting the paddles down and calling it.

The year of you can't save a marriage but maybe you can save
some other kind of partnership. The year of listening for what
you want and saying, Duty has run me around long enough.

Let the bar drop. Let the dishes wait and sink into rest like the
rest of them. Saturday—a thing you let happen to you—not just a
different list of tasks. A time, a window, of no tasks.

Let this be the year you try a little but also let the future reach
back to you. The year you wait for next. Actually. Learn. To.
Wait.

Waiting means no answers today. It means no road map for
this territory. Waiting is You Don't Have to Figure It Out Today.

Waiting is allowing the unfolding.

It's a new posture so you forget sometimes and look for
something to control, or you think it must be fixed or summoned
or created by your efforts alone, but this future doesn't work like
that. Maybe none of them ever did.

This is the year of loosening your grip, of long naps in the late
day sun. Of no emergencies, of everything is fixable except the
things that aren't and neither are a problem. One takes patience
and the other, acceptance.

I used to think it was all my responsibility. Bad things a
punishment and good things a reward.

But I was wrong.

The roof is leaking into my room when it rains, and my
bathtub drain is flooding floors below me.

But I am waiting for repair. I know it's the weekend, and these
things happen. They happen, and we repair them.

Acceptance.

This is the year of riding out a pandemic like a submarine in a storm. Plugging the holes. Then nothing to do but wait it out. Wait out the habits that broke us down or wore us out. Wait out the what will come and when. Wait out the rain and broken pipes and sour moods.

Surrender and sleep and small actions when we can. Tending our heart hearths. If nothing else, not letting this fire out. Stay warm. Stay here.

This is the year of getting through. Of sunlight on the floor when you can't get outside. Light through plant leaves. Beauty you would have skimmed over before, here for the savoring.

As it always, always was.

PM

It's peculiar to be sheltered in place because I feel sheltered inside, even smaller. When I talked to Laura and Jess the other day they talked about books they were reading and shows they were watching. It's hard to explain the way I have little appetite these days for the words or stories of others. I'm hungry for my own.

As if I could break down the door of "in here" like a row of movie characters swinging a giant log. Boom. Boom. BOOM. It opens and the treasure inside is yours.

What is the treasure?

Or if this is a mystery what is the question or the clue? What is waiting for me there?

And is it like a log swinging, really?

Tonight I feel more like a safe cracker, with a stethoscope in my ears. Turning the knob so gently, waiting for the "click".

I think I just wonder what's inside that I haven't been able to let myself see or willing to let myself know. I've been so committed to protecting the structure of my life, so committed to No Bombs Going Off, that heaven only knows what I buried in the cellar.

I remember feeling it after I started storytelling. Was it magnetism or the animal pull of my body. Or was it my own self, powerfully seen under a spotlight and heard behind a microphone? For years I thought I might explode. Instead I've created heart work-arounds and twisted myself into an elaborate pretzel. All to keep fitting inside this space.

So now there is something to untangle or there are pathways to iron out. I worry the pandemic's impact will be its own kind of confinement but that is not my business tonight. Tonight my business is to show up for the listening and the unraveling. To stop fighting all the things. Dharma, and the future, the agreements I made before coming earthside.

There is a place waiting for me but that is not relevant now. All that matters now is getting to the bottom of the bottom.

Finding the clues or answers or treasure behind the locked door.

What are you afraid of, that you would bury it there? All you ever wanted to find or to be was yourself. Yourself might defy words, or she might prefer polka dots and heels. I am here tonight, spinning the knob and listening for the click.

Left. Right. Left.

And maybe it's not a grand reveal or revelation. Maybe it's coming out one spoonful of soil at a time. There's some. There's some more. The feeling of dynamite powder under your feet and the way you've shied from power.

Click.

Sunday, May 10, 2020

What if I were to tell you my desk is very tidy these days but a pile of stuff is always sitting underneath it. That I need beauty right now but unsightly things, like this pile, are always sliding, spilling and persisting. The shiny bubble wrap envelope and books I keep meaning to read. A crimson Oklahoma University bath towel shoved under the place where the roof leaks down the wall.

What if I were to tell you my bathtub is full of coffee grounds and grains of rice from when he washed dishes yesterday. The pipes. Who knows what is up with them.

I was keeping my bed tidy so many days, but now—new piles there, too. Stationery for all the letters I mean to write. Maybe today.

But it makes visible, in a way, my inspiration. I sit in my bed surrounded by them. The slippers whose button I mean to sew back on. The torn shirt whose sleeves I mean to cut off. The bank statements I will turn into a budget.

I know I'm not the only one running low on execution. Even Moira in her great steadfastness feels it too.

But I wonder: What about putting something in a pile makes me think I will tend to it, when the opposite happens. Am I trying to make things easier for myself? "If the letters and stamps are already beside me when I wake, maybe the words will follow." And maybe it's true. Maybe it does serve as a reminder and maybe this will be the magical week I either do or shelve or cycle or finish them all, if only so I can stop being bothered by their clutter.

I do want things to be beautiful, but it's not worth appearing so if there is brokenness on the inside, water gushing through the walls. Now the rain stains down my bedroom wall just look like the truth.

What if I were to tell you I'm tired of moving and something in my heart feels spent there. I like knowing neighbors' names and it takes some time. I didn't know when I prepared this space for us that it would be the place we came apart. But maybe I did. I remember wanting it to be nice for the kids.

Noticing lately how I go overboard trying to tell or show my love for them instead of trusting them to know it, hold it, carry it. Or without finding out what speaks love to them. Over-serving them. So much offering and accommodating. "Want anything? Ice cream? Crackers? How about now?" Instead of leaving them space to feel their own hunger, in their own time. Instead of . . . I don't even know exactly what it looks like when I stop. But I'm trying to stop and say the thing under the thing.

"I think I just really want you to know I love you right now."

"I KNOW," they say.

Not yet, I think, but someday you might. And also? Maybe they do and I can trust them. Maybe I can try.

A word that captures the feeling of:

- Water is rushing through the walls and food is coming up the bath drain but I am taking it in stride.
- Some days in a global pandemic are easier than my life has been for a long time.
- I'm becoming the version of myself you always wished I would be.
- I've been holding things in so long, it's hard to shake them back out again.

Monday, May 11, 2020

The good news is that you are alive. Air rushing up your nose and lifting your ribs. Head held up by a nice solid wall. The good news is some of the houseplants are still alive. They get thirsty, lose leaves, and yet come back. Not afraid to drop their dead weight.

The good news is your pen is learning to keep moving even though it has no idea what's coming next. This is also you, moving through the day. Not knowing what's next but trusting something to come if you just keep going.

The good news is you're learning what love is just as quickly as you're learning what it's not. The good news is you'll probably be touched again. Someday.

The good news is the world is full of dear hearts and you will get to know and love a hundred more of them, in a hundred different ways.

The good news is there is more of you yet to be seen and discovered.

The good news is you're finding what you need—here inside of you. Sequestered even from friends and neighbors who are so often a shortcut to the connection you desire, to affection and joy. But here inside these walls they are yours to find the only place you carry with you—inside yourself.

This is correct and good and something to be grateful for. This time and this patience. So little to hurry along, so little to control for long enough that perhaps you can break the habit.

Here is what I've been trying to say. I don't know the future or what will come of this rapidly changing world. But I am learning myself. In the deep and inner core places. In ancient agreements. In forest clearings where it is finally time to dance.

What would dancing look like, and how would it feel? My hair flying about my face in slow motion, moonlight and fire light combining to release my power and inhibitions.

Here I am, mother. Here I am, old world and coming world. I am gathering like a storm and unleashing in a wild dance. Bare feet sinking in grass and soil and creation all around. Night creatures and invisible things and a music not outside me but inside.

This is your song, the stars say. We have been waiting for you, hum the trees.

Here I am, I say. There is nothing holding me back now, no one I must belong to, there are just white flowing garments and a flower crown and every hallelujah I have ever sung. Every prayer I have prayed and all the yes in my soul.

PM

Things you need before leaping into the unknown:

- A safety net. I'm so grateful for every dear heart who holds the net for me.
- A dream, even if you're missing the part you think should come with it—the steps from A to Z. Those are pipe dreams. This is more like a sonar ping saying, This way, or a metal detector on the beach imploring you to bring your shovel over here.
- You need to be done with the known, to have reached the end of what it has to offer. We love the known, for so many reasons, so this often requires a little shove.

A moment of clarity you can't unsee again. A longing you can't abide any longer. Or a pandemic. So many options here.

- You need the shoes or pants or jacket to step into it. This isn't about shopping, but about envisioning and inhabiting this next version of yourself. You just have to see it, and then put it on yourself. Belief. Confidence. No fucks left to give. Those garments have names like these.
- You will not fall forever, it just might feel that way. Somewhere a strong wind will come to lift you, or a place to land will appear to somersault onto.
- A feeling of no turning back as if jumping out the window of a house on fire. It's a commitment to leap. It's not a little dip of toes in the water.
- A good sense of timing. Not too early–there is something to wait for but I don't know if it's a voice or some just-right conditions. But it's not a panic bail, and it's also not waiting so long you miss the chance. For me the waiting is the hardest part.
- The vision which is like the dream, but maybe less intuition and more imagination. It's direction dressed up into something I can play in my mind. This is how it feels to come home in my new unknown: question mark question mark question mark. But damn that cup of tea I can imagine and leap into.
- Legs that know how to jump, a heart that keeps pumping and muscles that will stop trembling eventually, after you finally land.

Tuesday, May 12, 2020

It's been a time to take inventory. I have four unread books on
my shelf. Seems time to read or release them, but not continue
this piling up of intentions around me. Read, or let it go. It's
been so long since I've felt space to read. It's not about time—I'm
sure I've refreshed news sites long enough to have jammed out a
couple novels. It's more about not having space inside me to travel
elsewhere or take anyone else's stories in.

Our own stories have taken up so much room.

It's also been a time to visit other things, and perhaps this is its
own kind of inventory, too. Mapping an interior terrain.

Things that remind me of my mother:

- The song, *You Are My Sunshine*
- Doris Day
- molasses cookies

Or, Things I Might Have Done Differently which grows into
Things I Want to Do Better Next Time. Not some far-off next
time, in a wholly different setting with a different partner in
the mix. But next time like this morning when the kitchen was
crowded and I chose to be soft instead of hostile. The kind of
Next Time that can start right now because it's about me, and
my learning will certainly keep growing but it is also present and
now.

How we run from the inventory and the reflection. How much
easier to hide things behind closet doors and leave them there.
Our coat closet is currently in this state of disaster.

It's time to rotate out spring coats and shoes for winter ones,
except there's not much need for such things this year. I got

the kids summer shoes in one of my last urgent feats before the Staying Home, but now I can see they may not leave even the apartment for so long the shoes may be outgrown again by then.

It is a strange time. And one struggles to rate tasks by urgency or importance because we realize we never understood these concepts, or perhaps they've just been turned on their heads. Working the piles is something I can do this week, and so I am.

I keep thinking of this time Amelia came up to the roof with me, during our first month at home. The sky was bright and the sun was afternoon-shining. We said the ways we feel prepared for this time by our experiences these last six months, and also three years.

We were already disrupted, and undone. Already facing a future we couldn't quite imagine and dealing with matters of life and death. It felt like already living in a land called Uncertainty and simply being joined there.

Wednesday, May 13, 2020

Sometimes it feels like somersaulting through time, the way the days twist in and out and around you. Awake in the night, morning waking three times before rising. Dinnertime just when it felt like midday and finally getting to your words once night has covered the windows.

There is time for watching but also listening. Sometimes the listening is like excavation and other times it's like waiting for something to rise to the top.

Maybe it's wanting things to matter that drives so much action and activity. Wanting the day to matter, and ourselves moving through it.

Actually it's just something I put on myself. Wanting *me* to matter.

It's all so interesting to observe, like a forced retreat, without the solitary and silent part. But something in me is sequestered and the other parts are observing all my machinery in motion.

Sometimes it feels like missing my people terribly, but other times it feels like carrying them so seamlessly inside me I don't register things like distance or absence.

Sometimes it feels like a great dismantling or rearranging, sometimes being reduced to my most common denominator and sometimes it feels like I am a puzzle being put back together. Sometimes it feels like time for bed but the sleep memo didn't get through, just the memory projector playing through as if with a mind of its own.

Ribs. Always I am remembering ribs. Rising falling. That large expansive motion right before words come tumbling out. Ribs like a whale's with myself trapped inside at sea. Ribs around me. Memory machine now projecting on the interior walls of the whale.

Ribs like heart protection. Like breath bellows. Ribs like a drum that is beat from the inside.

Boom boom. Boom boom.

Ribs and everything I hold inside them. Every scent and deep breath and spring breeze and all the tenderness inside them. My soft places. Heart space and breath house.

Sometimes it feels like ribs, my own rising and falling or head resting on another's strong wall.

Sometimes it feels somatic in a way I love. Even the memories are embodied. Looking at my body and wondering if I am anyone else's memory—this hair or laugh or smile.

Tonight I am floating. I am still in a belly, out at sea, so, of course I am. Of course I am.

Thursday, May 14, 2020

I don't want to forget how much changing I'm doing on the inside. The way we buy a Lucky Charms/Frosted Flakes combo now. How I'm letting go of putting judgments on things and this hierarchy of value. Like kale is greater than toast is greater than cookies. Or like: creating with physical objects is better than creating virtually. Like: screen time is the enemy and being controlling is good parenting in the end.

What if it isn't? What if it's not worth it to try and shape the children or make them turn out the way we wish they would? What if all that efforting has unintended consequences that take years or decades of undoing?

I'm trying a new way now. Maybe it will explode, too. Maybe the kids will turn out disastrously. But aren't we all a beautiful disaster, each in our own ways?

This new way is called: I trust you to listen to yourself. It's called: I will hold you with acceptance and a great friendliness. It's called: I will stop hovering and overly servicing your wants and anticipating your needs and calling it love.

It's called: Everyone here is old enough to learn how to take care of themselves. Gently, without being under a microscope. As if freshman year of college starts now. I remember eating a Snickers bar once for breakfast my freshman year and it tasted like independence and freedom. Why must it wait until then?

I will give reminders, gentle ones for meals and afternoon snacks and bedtime. But I will roll responsibility more to them. This feels correct. I'm dreaming of doing it in more ways, still— like color-coded dishes for each person—but this is good enough for now. It's a start.

It's strange to create space for autonomy and not worry about it crushing togetherness, like having one's own shelf in the pantry.

But isn't this how people negotiate being good roommates? Or sharing a workplace fridge? Having boundaries helps us be together—this is my hypothesis. My current, imperfect idea.

PM

Things You Might Need to Hear Before Bed
1. Some things probably happened today, but you can read about them tomorrow.
2. Some people are working on problems. Some are trying very hard. We can all do our part, and this sometimes takes humility. Some days our part looks bigger or smaller but it's ours, just the same. Live the day.
3. And you did. You lived this one. The world was lucky to have you here in it.
4. However you feel tonight, others felt it, too. They wrote it into a song, or had no words for it at all. But others were beside you whether you could see and hear them or not.

Imagine all of you in a sacred circle, sending each other some tenderness.

5. If you found the words someone else found, now is a good time for them. You really can keep reading that one book again and again, and then let the author's voice do the same, until you don't need it traveling beside you any longer. Same for albums. Films. Songs.

6. Your beautiful body carried you through this day or at least kept your heart beating. Snaps for the bodies. (And maybe some moisturizer.)

7. Tomorrow is a new day. Your eyes will open into it if you are lucky and you will be a whole day wiser than you were today.

8. The new day will be what it is and you will be however you are in it and the two of you will tango or hug it out.

9. You are beloved, and irreplaceable.

10. A bit of sleep now is all you need. Try and drink it like something delicious and refreshing. *Ahh.* Or, it can cover you like a blanket. Either way, it's for you.

Friday, May 15, 2020

It's hard to track what's changed because they aren't only visible, external things.

We ask different questions. "Where do we go from here?" feels less useful than "Where we are now?"

We ask different things. We expect something else of our days—no longer shaped by a rhythm of outings, destinations or adventures. Now a day is largely framed by food. We prepared, we ate, we cleaned up. Or at least I did.

The days have a new kind of predictability. I will listen to the news over coffee. Linus will help wake the kids. I will remind everyone when it's time to make lunch. I will have a phone call or conversation that may breathe some life into me. My work mind may start rebooting, but then it will be time to help with a school assignment. Then time to start dinner, run a bath, go to bed.

Repeat repeat repeat.

There is something lovely in the repetition—something comforting in at least this small measure of knowing what's coming. In this way it feels different than a true war zone, where bombs could anytime rain from the sky.

So much unknown and yet enough reason to believe tomorrow will likely look much like today. This was the assurance the world lost so collectively these last months. But in my family we have lost this one before.

I often think of my artist-mom friend Mel after her family returned to their native Australia after years in Brooklyn. "It's amazing how fast one adapts," she said. "Two weeks later I'm in line at the DMV here, clearly a world apart from there, and yet our days already have a new sense of rhythm."

It's like that, she taught me. We have that adaptability in us. It takes a small time, it's true, but we are lovers of rhythms and rituals here. It is held with softness and flex but in this small way we imagine a future.

I cannot tell you about September. But I can make some solid predictions about tomorrow, and next week.

And that's something. Today it's enough.

Saturday, May 16, 2020

PM

Tell me again how strong we are. About stacking days and how far we have come. Remind me of the good land to plant trust in. Take me back to the place it all started. The first reaching out for the future and the first yes across our terrestrial lips.

Tell me once more about love. How it is like an element in the atmosphere. An animating force.

Tell me again it's okay to feel it all, all the way. Even the parts that feel jagged and sharp. Even the ones that feel like a bottomless canyon where one's heart used to be. The ones that feel heavy, and the ones flying about like live wires.

The ones that make a body go completely still, or explode into action.

Tell me a story about how nothing means anything but it all matters so much. In low, quiet tones say thoughts so thick I have to sigh into them.

Remind me of the things that will not change. Stars on a clear night. The feeling of someone beside me, even in that way that is untouched by space and time.

In some quiet field where the only sound is birdsong, our

dearest ones are planted deep inside us and have taken root.
A whole grove of unending loves to shade us, or whisper
reassurances above our heads in the breeze.

Here even in the not here. This is the mystery. One we cannot
easily shake, even if we try.

Here in the not here. Love like atmosphere, like breath. Roots
and leaves and the ground we came from. The ground we will all
someday return to.

Tell me my name again. Not just the I Am Called one, but my
true name. The one spoken by deities and stars that says who I
am in the great universe of things, beings, and beloveds.

I am always forgetting, but you never do.

Monday, May 18, 2020

One way to become is to let yourself be undone. Unlaced.
Unraveled. Like all those objects or products you use to contain
or control your hair—pulled out, tossed aside. Au naturel.

What is the blank slate version of your body, un-fussed
over? What is the blank slate version of your mind, with all
the assumptions or expectations abandoned along the way. Or
washed down the sink.

What if all this becoming or presenting has actually carried
your further into the land of efforting. What if they have won
you over into new illusions of How to Get There or How to Be a
Good *Fill in the Blank*.

What if it was all a ruse, or misguided in the least. What if all this effort pulled you away from other kinds of becoming, like:

Emerging. Rising from ashes or opening, in one's own time, like a bloom.

Or unlearning. Untrying. Hearing the old scripts bubble up to your lips and deciding: No thank you I will now try a new way.

A new way to love, to parent, to allow us all more space to be. To feel our own rhythms and follow them. To be unscrutinized. To let the hovering sheep dog go.

This weekend I took long naps two days in a row. I had the worry that always follows rest: Am I depressed?

No, a gentle reminder graciously found me.

You are healing.

One way to love yourself is to find your breath and follow it. What next? Water. How about now? Air.

All this looking, all these years, to the outside for the answers the way the direction or guidance. When there is actually something that feels like a fountain inside me, wanting to bubble up to the surface through my cheeks, my eyelids, to slip out of the gap between my teeth just before words form.

What if this is becoming: letting so many so many things go. Or maybe it's letting them be. Myself most of all.

Myself. Most of all.

Tuesday, May 19, 2020

I don't want to write about the times I get lost in a sister life, some other path I didn't take. Or maybe it's fantasy or maybe just a dream. Is the thing I long for even real?

Could kindness be a way of life? How about understanding, or affection? Could my body drape across another's frame in a way that feels like safety or coming home? Are these experiences just fleeting moments or are they a land one could live in?

Will there be another chance to be cherished, or companioned.

We sink even deeper into our own solitudes as the days pile up. Longer between messages, less reaching out, or maybe finally recalibrating what we can support. In the beginning it felt frenzied—this desire to sustain togetherness. But it was unsustainable.

Perhaps something slower now, some letter writing, perhaps. Shorter messages, more frequently.

The way I'm pulling the idea of being a connected or disconnected person out from being in a relationship or not. The way the two don't go together the way people assume.

So I don't want to write about other days I dream of, either future or past. I want to be all here, but it's confusing to rework one's relationship with time. I'm a happy resident of my World Inside a World. Most of the time.

But I'd be lying if I didn't say I also dream of another chapter after this one. Of community and neighbors around my table. I dream of beach walks and sweet togetherness. Being appreciated, enjoyed, and every now and then even celebrated.

It's not useful to dwell on what's missing right now, except to feel out the shape of what might someday be. All my memories and experiences are still mine, I still carry them with me like a gift I got to keep even after everything changed.

We are in a strange in-between now. But I am letting myself sit just a bit in the waiting. Wishing I had more bandwidth for hustling but also losing my appetite for it. I think I'm in the healing.

And the healing will release me when it's good and ready.

Wednesday, May 20, 2020

Let's start here. Weather warm enough for bare toes on the beam beneath the table. How he says the days there are up and down, too. For a moment of hope that made me cry.

Let's start here. With a day I feel stronger in, revived from yesterday, and walking with my face in the sun. Heeled boots and how I forgot the way they are nice to walk in.

Let's start here, a homemade peppermint mocha in oatmilk and the real camera out for a black and white life photography challenge. Let's start with returning to the editing room to put a young artist on display.

Or let's start here. With my beloved friend at the doctor today and the way I thought it was tomorrow and messaged her something incorrect at the time she needed me to get it right. I hope she is resting and not angry. Most of all I hope she didn't get bad news while I was going on about less important things.

The way I'm always trying to be a good *fill in the blank* but especially a good friend. It's the one role I feel I have a shot at landing, so when I stumble on that ground I am extra ashamed.

Let's start here with the mocha flavor settling at the bottom of my cup and the way I want something to settle inside me, too. A concentration of flavor that is underneath every other sip. The way it is undiluted by all this milk and swirling like its own art through the remnants at the bottom of my mug-well.

Drink deeply, it says. Not just of this beverage but the most You parts of yourself.

Let's start here. Learning not to obscure myself but swirl without self-consciousness. To be tasted and revive the hearts of all who drink.

Let's start here, with trusting words to come as the pen moves and direction to arrive as I listen. Here in the now, as I invite my imagination to assemble a sweet future to walk into next. Ready, set. Let's start here and now.

Thursday, May 21, 2020

Here we go. No pistols firing at the starting place. No balloons or cheers or homemade signs shouting positive phrases.

Here we go, with just a little now-cold coffee in the bottom of the cup. No one and nothing waiting on you precisely, at a given hour, but plenty populating the day's list.

Might as well begin now. Begin with a soft blue cover and these lined pages and the way your mother knew it would be better if it laid flat when opened.

Might as well write with a hand already feeling strain, a reminder one can complete motions without such a grip.

Here we go, not just into a day called Thursday, as if it were its own flavor of days in an ice cream shop's seven-day rotation. As if there have not been scores of Thursdays in the past. Did they always taste differently than Tuesdays?

So much these days tastes the same.

Or the opposite—slightly foreign in our mouths. Is this what tater tots really tasted like, before?

Before we bought them in Flatbush, before only one store in our radius carried this shape. Before they came in a stark white bag with black block letters and a splash of red?

Did we always know the trick of cooking them longer and hotter to get crispy? I think we just mastered it last night but this like so many things, we could have figured out so long ago.

Here we go now, nice and easy like a box of hair dye says. Noticing the way nice is a word let go of long ago. It's not nice, not for anything.

So here we go, fierce and easy and drifting and marching. Here we go, swaying or singing. Here we go with ohs and ahs rising and falling. Here we go with enough ink for this day, with paper to hold it. Here we go with lips licked and brows furrowed and the way you rock yourself into it, like something very beloved, like something wanting to be gathered, as into arms.

Here.

We.

Go.

PM

Things I Am Hungry For:

1. The way my mother smells when my arms are around her neck.
2. My friends and the way the light falls on them, the way they fill the space beside me.
3. Cocoa. Cocoa. More cocoa. A splash of peppermint inside.
4. The feeling things might work out in the end.
5. The nearness of a person who makes my body come alive.
6. Something from where I came from. The stories from my childhood that feel most true.
7. My grandmother's fingers interlaced in mine.
8. Something deep and knowing in my low belly that helps me to believe.
9. Scones and tea.
10. Maggie's good company and the stairway tile in Sterling Place.
11. Lucy's good night kisses when they're feeling soft and generous.
12. A future I could imagine.
13. But still: just a little more quiet. Just a little more solitude. I don't want to miss this now by wishing or rushing away.
14. The kind of purpose that ignites me. Vitality that surfs me along its way.
15. Kindness. Gentleness.
16. Someone who can say, "I know just what you need."
17. Or, "Come here."
18. A grassy spot I could lay in on a starry night.

19. Reminders of gravity. Here I am here I am and not floating
     away into the atmosphere.
20. Anything—a flowy dress, or a glance—the color of love.

Friday, May 22, 2020

"What if I'm lost?" is a question I ask myself at 4:30 in the
morning, with a noisy kitty disturbing my slumber.

I'm learning the sound of my own doubt. It has a certain
chorus: What if I'm doing it wrong? And the family is breaking,
or the children are in distress?

What if I missed my work moment, trying to hold what I
thought was My Life together? Tried holding my heart together
through loss after loss and so many interruptions.

What if my marketing funnel got clogged or I accidentally
threw it out with the recycling.

What if I missed it. Fell behind. Got it wrong.

Like a car veering to avoid a small animal and ending up
crumpled in a ditch instead. What if in trying to avert disaster
I've only created a bigger mess?

This is the sound of my anxiety.

Next, I come rushing to my own rescue with Great New Plans.
We will have a family meeting, we will talk in a Feelings Circle.

We will heal at last. Live in peace. Smile at each other in the
morning when we are still groggy.

I quickly come up with similar plans for work. I will Boost
The Signal and write my email list and sit at the laptop every day.

I will let people see the things I make. I will get out of my own way.

I will emerge—finally—as Just The Thing You Were Hoping For. The Just What You Need When You Can't Sleep at Night. I will be Just The Thing for Your Friend, Too.

I will be for everyone.

It will be easy. So easy I throw back my head during interviews and laugh.

"All I am doing is what I've done all along!" I will chuckle at the world's surprised discovery of me, as if it has finally gotten my joke.

As if I'm the last one at Hide and Seek to be found.

"Silly friends," my amused smile in dramatic portraits will say. "I was here all along."

Like someone dressed to match the wallpaper, finally stepping forward with a small wave. Is this what it's like to be found?

Or could it also happen in the grass, lying in a row of graves.

Couldn't it also happen when someone loves you enough to let you say the hard things, to get them wrong, to choke on tears the whole way through so you keep having to repeat your words to be understood.

Could it be a moment in a bed alone, when you are not afraid of the aloneness.

Couldn't it also be the way feet feel sliding into slippers, or the warm trail tears leave running down your cheeks.

Maybe it could be saying the thing that might lose you love, and playing the hand all the way through.

Being found might be in the colleague's voice saying: You're not invisible even after all this time.

All the calendars of strong-feeling days mixed with foggy ones.
You thought it was an equation, all your efforts adding up
to something. But it was really your feet exploring forest floor,
looking for a path.

PM

I ask my sister, What do you do when your husband is on the
roof, on the phone, telling his mother about your divorce?
I am making cocoa and lying down.

"I should record some videos," I say to my daughter, "while my
hair is clean." She can see I'm struggling to lift my head.

"It will be clean again another day," she assures me. I decide she
is right. A cup of Lady Gray tea props my head up until a pre-
dinner bath.

A bath before dinner is a sure sign of A Day. At least for me.

I am listening to a song called "Lucky One" by La Force and
thinking of people who have loved me before. I don't know the
words but it feels like my mood just now.

I would like to rock gently, forward and back and then side
to side. To submerge in warm water that makes me say, "Oh my
god" out loud. Every time. My inner frog essence, happy to be
back in its element.

I would like to look back on this time someday as a rebirth
of sorts. The part of the movie where the music picks up and in
a montage that makes your hand fly up to your chest our main
character becomes the heroine of her story.

Go girl, we whisper.

Inside the montage, life feels slow. One piece of good news
immediately countered by the evening news reports.

But my encouraging email! My possibility! My story, gestating inside me for a someday screen!

I cannot hold it present all the time. Sometimes I have to sit on hold with the insurance company for an hour with no answers. I need to start the pizza crust even though I have no appetite for Friday night.

This one feels depressingly like a Wednesday. A rainy one at that.

Anyway the bathwater won't stay hot forever. Time to climb in.

Saturday, May 23, 2020

It's a time for new clothes. Not just to suit our fancy or entertain a craving for newness, the missing shopping expeditions to signal the arrival of spring or fall. But new clothes because we are changed, even in our bodies.

It calls for a great gentleness as we change sizes. An inner dictum that demands we love these bodies just as much—if not more—than the ones we lived in before.

We have learned to acknowledge our hunger, our cravings and appetite. We've learned to not place judgments like clean or dirty or healthy or junk onto our food.

We are learning what it feels like to be nourished. To let ourselves take up space.

To be fed.

We are learning to care for ourselves like rhythm, like a

pendulum on a grandfather clock, even when the humidity pushes our appetite away. Even when life makes our taste buds dull.

We are learning to swallow our care in small bites, to show up unfailingly, in high moods and in low ones.

We are learning to hold our softness without apology.

All our softness. Cheeks that pull into smiles, arms that invite beloveds into them, hearts that feel every expression and modulation of tone like earthquakes or ocean breezes.

In this season, we let ourselves want what we want, without judgment or apology. It is no time for rationing anything that feeds us.

We are still learning to allow ourselves a full portion.

We are learning there can be enough for everyone, that there could be more where this came from. That if apple juice feels good right now, then apple juice it will be.

We order a few new-to-us things for our new summer and we shuffle around new garments and old ones with each other. Maybe this is for you, now.

I love us soft, and I love us strong. We have never been so beautiful.

PM

My Discover Weekly playlist is dead on tonight. It's time for sleep, or reading before sleep, but I want the sounds to keep washing over me. It's like ocean waves in the form of a chord progression.

Linus is curled up in the space between my legs. He sees the pen and keeps wondering if it's something he should pounce on.

Today it's hard not to reach out to the past. Already I've done too much, sent one message I regret. Looked up articles on how to stop doing that. "Don't reach out for comfort in the place you lost it," one said.

Much emotional energy spent today and no outward forward motion. I asked Amelia, "Is this what rest feels like?" and took a nap at 5pm. The long light is affecting our body rhythms for sure.

My eyes are watering with weariness. What am I hoping to reach so late?

I miss all the togetherness I've ever had. Maybe that's it. I miss the places in which I was wanted. I covet the moments where it felt like cylinders falling into place, like being in just the right place at the right time. My first time behind the microphone.

It's very likely I am still in the dead center of where I belong, and right on schedule. I am ready to step out, and ready to be received.

Trust. Rest. Trust some more.

Sunday, May 24, 2020

Today I will pray the headache lifts, the teeth will stay in place and not fall out like they want to when it gets like this.

Today I will walk to my old home and sit in the garden with Maggie. We will order burrito bowls for lunch. Maybe we will really go crazy and add chips to the list.

Today I will remember moments of sweetness and try to believe they are mine forever in a way that edges out the sorrow that they couldn't last longer. I have known sweetness, I will tell my arms and their phantom memories. I have known love. I have seen the gleam of delight in eyes that beheld me. Not everyone is so blessed.

Not everyone is so blessed. What an interesting ground to stand on, like the painted white circles now painted through our park lawns. One could pick another circle. A tragic or feeling sorry for oneself one. Or one could stand here.

Stand in appreciation and gratitude. Stand in hope for sweet days to come without missing the sweetness in this one.

Here's what I'm trying to say. I don't have to forget anything, I can make space for even the most wrenching parts. I just want to transform them somehow so instead of broken shards of glass under my feet they become seeds that travel deep into my soil, and live there. Maybe growing into something new or just resting peacefully, marked by a small headstone and an occasional bouquet.

Here's what I also want to say. Please let this body not fight me forever. Let there come a day when it lets me be. May I be strong enough to press through and humble enough to go easy until then.

May the sun and trees be a salve today. Let me find comfort in Maggie's good company, even though there are hard words to say. May I find relief in the not having to keep saying them that will come someday.

Let music wash over me like a bath with special sea salts that make one's skin silky, with minerals seeping into pores and reviving me. I am in need of revival.

There are so many days ahead.

Monday, May 25, 2020

Inspired by "It Doesn't Have to Be Beautiful" by Cynthia Berg

It doesn't have to be beautiful. The bedroom window could stay dirty another day. The rust colored trails from ceiling down to floor can remain until the roof is finally, finally fixed.

It doesn't have to be beautiful. My hair, frizzy for today's camera because I didn't put the second product on last night.

And maybe the jumpsuit can be, without alterations for my less than medium-sized chest, and I could just enjoy it.

Just like that: my whole to do list for the day out the window. *It doesn't have to be beautiful* frees up so much time I wonder what I'll do with it.

Permission granted to sit in the corner of this bed I have not learned how to spread across yet. Permission granted to find some words, to gaze out windows. To let the debris exhale for a moment before I clear it all away.

Permission granted to make a warm drink. To dwell in the kids' room awhile. To let my mind rest in this way that's yet unclear, like an appetite unsure of what it wants for dinner.

My wanting wants to finish the story Tabitha and I are watching. To feel it one hundred percent and all the way.

My wanting wants to remember being loved as a way of hoping it into my future.

My wanting wants to let new notes wash over me and it wonders if some notes would like to come out of me.

My wanting wants to tell the story and sing the song, except when my wanting wants to be very quiet and very still while the story and song are weaving together inside me.

My wanting wants my lower abdomen to feel well, like it isn't holding too much, or lacking too greatly, either. For that part of my body to cease its trembling.

My wanting wants softness today. Rest as an ingathering of strength, but without such an agenda, or really any at all. Not rest because I walked three hours yesterday or because tomorrow is coming. Rest simply because my wanting wants it, and I can trust that alone. A complete sentence.

No justification required.

Wednesday, May 27, 2020

Where I'm from we get what we deserve. Goodness, a sign of virtue, and mishaps or misfortunes evidence of our lack of diligence at best, or our sin, at worst.

Where I'm from we pray blessings over our meals. We squeeze the hands we're holding in a circle a few times, gently like a heartbeat—*boom boom, boom boom*—before letting go.

Where I'm from the beauty of the mountains is there whether you can see it today or not.

Where I'm from, mothers kiss little foreheads and dream of new ways to convince people of our love, or deposit our affection inside so it could carry or fuel them forever. So it will not be forgotten, even after we are gone.

Where I'm from you don't take too much in case there's not enough to go around. You make three pans of bread dressing to accommodate everyone.

Where I'm from wives are the helpers, along for the ride. They sometimes give up their own journey for some other kind of security.

We are held, until we aren't.

Where I'm from girls are told they can do anything and then spend decades wondering why life doesn't agree.

If we get what we deserve, the fault must lie with us. We must not have been *fill in the blank* enough. Bright enough to be hired. Beautiful enough to be desired. Compliant enough to be kept.

Where I'm from we keep our promises. We don't give up. We give up our very own selves before we ever quit. *Sacrifice your body!* is the mantra we learned about risking injury to slide into home base. It rings in our ears in too many other moments, too.

Where I'm from a pink house on a Colorado/Kansas border has a pink bathtub inside. The only toys are small plastic buckets with strings one walks on like stilts.

The old ladies' skin folds into lines and creases, and the part on the backs of their hands grows thin. The old men are already gone.

Where I'm from we would rather spare your feelings than tell the truth. Truth is for behind people's backs, for side conversations. Truth is kept under the table, passed sideways like a wordless glance or a side dish no one particularly wants.

Where I'm from we love so hard it might be our undoing. Might split us open. Finally. Please.

Afternoon

Today the roofers came to fix the leak that causes it to rain inside my bedroom. It's been fixed so many times it's hard to get my hopes up. "Thanks for coming," I can say. "Thanks for trying."

A whole day watching their gear suspended down exterior walls. Feet outside my room for hours, each foot wrapped in a plastic shopping bag—one black, one white.

Do you fix other things, I want to ask, thinking of other places we feel ourselves raining on the inside. I have stopped, though. Trying to mend everything or believing it's always possible.

Tonight I box up old dishes and make way for new ones. I will try the new dress tomorrow and hope it fits.

But today was for insurance and providers. For falling prey to fraud and contacting authorities. For hours on hold and transfer to this department, then that one, and the other.

Today was for simply getting through. Nothing extra, no flying colors. It was for mourning the news and the way systems of oppression poison us all. A double pandemic in our midst.

For chores that never cease and heat that makes us droop. Not just heat but humidity—its thickness in the air.

Today is for saying There Are No Words Today just bare minimum steady motion. For almost dinner, maybe on new plates. The old ones taking up so much room in boxes. I won't know where to put them. But I know I can't be overwhelmed by our collective mess anymore and I cannot keep thinking of the past.

Today is for trying to still believe in the future that wants me, even though today it means Not Giving Up and also No Decisions.

Today is for just a few more dishes and moving things out of sight.

For almost dinner, then bedtime and maybe something to lift my spirits in between.

Friday, May 26, 2020

After the roof leaked again and again.
After hours spent in rooms with therapists.
After hitting the dead end of: I love you but not the way a husband should.

After starting over. Again. And again. After three moves in two years. After letting go of my possessions to follow someone else's dream.

After farewells and heartbreaks.

Anchor after anchor pulled up from my ocean floor. After nights praying in the courtyard with my palms against tree trunks. After wanting what I cannot have. After dinner-cooking and dishwashing. After 21 years.

After illnesses stemming from stress. After living with anger or abandonment on repeat. After lonelier than I've ever been.

After he tried to convince himself I'm pretty. After he couldn't remember love as a reason he chose me.

After coming alive. After expanding and still trying to fit inside one person's fixed view of me.

After knowing I'm part of the problem. After buying a home and adopting a kitten. After finally feeling some steady ground underfoot.

A new unraveling begins.

It's easy to worry the best is behind me, that I won't be seen or known again. It's easy to think this part of my story is ending. It's easy to catastrophize about the future and have bad dreams about my worst case scenarios.

But I'd rather start here than end here. I'd rather be brave and believing than a damsel in distress or a tragic figure. The Discarded Housewife.

I'd rather rise and unfold my full wingspan and thrive in a space that does not discount or treat me as invisible. I would like to come to my own rescue.

Before the path reveals. Before the provision arrives or the miracle made manifest, there is the believing. There is one small action after another. There is resting and regrouping. Allowing a new dream to dream us. A new future to weave and reach back to us.

Before the next is the now. Our own lips shaping the sound, yes. Our own heart open to possibility, daring to want something and to speak the wanting out loud.

Before the end is the rest of the story. The new chapter, the next act. Curtain falling, then rising again.

Saturday, May 27, 2020

Right now birdsong mingles with sirens. A large bee flies between gravestones. Surely these bird calls are communicating something and right now I wish I knew what they were saying.

If I were a bird right now, I'd say: Isn't the light pretty like this, when the sun drops back down to the side of the sky? If I were a bird right now I wouldn't know much about human problems. I'd feel the seasons in their rhythm and do the things my body simply knew to do.

Right now it's Saturday and I'm weary but sometimes rest looks like green leaves against blue sky and my eyes here to see them, my ears here to hear the chorus they make in the breeze.

Right now I sit under a favorite tree in the company of my "dead friends" as Amelia called them as I left. I'm sitting near some Coppolas and thinking about movies. I'm sitting in the presence of death and thinking about life.

Right now these words feel like a great effort. Right now I wish my friends and I were holding each other. Right now I wish the future felt like a thing one could imagine or envision and sculpt from clay.

Right now history reminds us we are at a single dot on an immense timeline. Space reminds us we occupy one rock orbiting through a vast darkness, organized around one of countless stars.

Right now I'd give anything for a drink from my coffee shop. Soon, perhaps.

But first there is just Mama Earth and me resting my body in a sliver of shade. Right now just this body, aching for rest, relief, repeat.

There will be so many more days to work and fight for justice. There will be days to execute and upload.

I do not know what comes next and I do not even dare to guess. But right here no other moment matters. Just these birds. This breeze. A dropping sun and a chorus of songs.

June 2020

Wednesday, June 3, 2020

What it looks like:

Another night with my head held up by the wall behind my bed, weak with weariness and aching. A whole day without underwear because I needed to do the wash and forgot. It looks like feeling so busy and wall-to-wall occupied from beginning of day to the end but wondering what there is to show for it. A couple posts or petitions signed—is that all? How was there not more reading, or walking, or underwear laundering?

I don't know.

It looks like the insurance company calling with the authorization code. Like Lucy crying because they don't know they are capable of a ten page essay yet.

It's my friend's heart breaking before breakfast. The sound of her chopping something in the kitchen as she recounted the story.

It looks like Grandpa J emailing us memories from 1968. I want all the stories.

I want to see my grandparents again.

And my friends.

Sometimes it feels this era will never end, and yet every day is a new world right now. As if our life is a play unfolding on a stage and different backgrounds keep dropping down behind us.

It's a year of Getting a Bigger Problem, again and again. The imagination doesn't even want to extrapolate it out from here.

The question now is not how to save our institutions or systems but how best to dismantle and rebuild them. There is deep learning and wild imagining to do.

But there will also be stories to tell, both of what's so and of

what's possible. I am here for that. I don't understand much else
these days, and pre-scheduled work is hard to execute even as I
feel a deadline coming Friday.

Each day just doing what I can, in a throwing-the-ball-from-
half-court-at-the-buzzer way.

Thursday, June 4, 2020

I have lost my appetite for so many things. Introspection of the
kind I was doing before this before and not the before before that
one, feels unimportant and has been replaced with more pressing
and important things.

Mostly I keep thinking of this thing people I once knew used
to say. If someone became overwhelmed with a challenge in front
of them, they would say, "You need a bigger problem." The
idea being that a "bigger problem" has a way of pulling things
back into perspective. That parking ticket seems like a real day
wrecker until the doctor calls with worse news. That's the idea.

And what's handy is, it works, in a bizarre way.

I keep thinking of it because it's felt like the season of Getting
a Bigger Problem and having others recede. In my personal life,
for sure. But now in the world outside, too.

Can you even remember what our biggest problem was before
the pandemic? Honestly who knows. And we thought that was
rough. Now our bigger problems of systemic racism have people
taking to the street in droves, in every state, in countries across

the globe, risking transmission of a potentially deadly virus because We Have Bigger Problems.

The truth is I have little to say because living takes a lot right now. And I am doing what I am doing and there is no reason to write about those things.

Here's what I want you to know. This is a moment and we are alive in it. It's important to pay attention, because what we do right now is something we will look back on.

I do not know all the things and I do not get it all right. Just today my daughter pointed out how in my parenting, my attempts to help aren't helping. I can hear it and I can learn. And these things are being asked of us in public life, too. The two of us laughed and laughed at my failure. We came back to it later, and laughed some more.

How we try. How what we think loving or caring or helping looks like and how far off is our aim.

I will be learning to do better until I leave this life.

Saturday, June 6, 2020

In no particular order, Amelia waits for hot water and I wait to message my grandparents until getting words down here.

Police officers in Flatbush covering their badge numbers with black tape.

The birds singing in the courtyard. Police sirens going by and the way it makes us tense and jumpy now.

Dishes waiting, sheets bleaching, untold stories rising up my throat like heartburn.

My head hurting another day. The world hurting another day and perhaps my body is simply a receiver tuned into the frequency.

The way heartbeats of things can stop. Relationships. But maybe also paradigms. Maybe we really can strangle out the broad acceptance of injustice if not every last ember.

The emotional expense of rage, our bodies unconditioned to this much sorrow.

The graves in the graveyard and the way they remind me I'm still alive.

So what will I do? What. Will I. Do with it. I am answering in tiny ways but it's clear they are just a foot-tap to the music. They are not really joining the dance yet. I'm watching and learning with my eyes: What are the dance steps and how do they go?

I'm tuning my ear to hear on a new frequency, dial up and down honing in on the melody that's been drowned by static.

And I'm trying to feel the music in my body. Steps be known but also steps be damned as I let the part inside that wants to join emerge. To learn and follow, yes, but from a deep in my bones true way.

In an "I can't hear this beat another minute longer and not stand up" way. Even as I look for my place in the room.

Chairs have no place in this song.

Sunday, June 7, 2020

The way I only realized tonight in the bath how it's affected my body. The violence we've witnessed by police.

All weekend listening for words I need. Delegitimize. Mobilize. The breaking of the social contract. Fraternity over justice. The words swim through my mind as someone sets off fireworks in the courtyard, each one a sound blast that makes me jump while a light pink or white light bounces off the building blocks.

The way it sits in my abdomen and the muscles and fascia tremble to hold the things they carry now. Fear. Acceptance. Sorrow. Shock.

The feeling of losing one belief system after another. Every time, the way I feel foolish for believing—for wanting the thing to be true so badly we ignore evidence to the contrary. Things like Freedom and Justice for All.

But this trembling in my abdomen, this twitchiness in my muscles like voltage, even though it's late. Even though it's bedtime.

Friends who let me say it again and again and again.

My breath, shallow, like there isn't room for it down deep.

Monday, June 8, 2020

You could start here, wiggling in a kitchen chair, trying to get comfortable. Here, in your restlessness that would rather walk than write. You could start here, after a morning spent finding out the bank closed your account.

With the wanting to give up.

And whatever that might prove. That the system was rigged or the stars were against you. That your hopes were "airy fairy" like cotton candy and not anything to live off of. That dreams and work can't sustain you?

It doesn't prove anything to give up, not today.

You could start here, in the regrouping and in the listening. You could start even now, with a prayer. A small action, not even meant to be The Action but something more like a flare launched into the sky.

Dear Future, I am here. I am here looking for you and hoping you are there looking for me.

I don't believe in angels in the same way I used to but I still require belief in some kind of something.

Light flare. Wait. Repeat.

Try on another day to build my own rescue vehicle. Today brainstorming ideas.

What do I build to get from here to there? A raft? A glider?

Hard to say when the destination is unclear.

Let's start here. A forehead resting on a hand and light coming through the window. Let's start with rest, maybe. Or imagination. Or thinking or organization, whatever bubbles up next.

Let's start in the discouragement. In the weary and uncertain.

Let's not run from it. Feet dangling, Lucky Charms remnants still on the table.

My heart, still beating. My heart still beating.

Still dreaming and listening and waiting. What if no day was a sidetrack or a "wash"? What if every situation had its role to play? Would I let myself be shaped, be taught?

Tuesday, June 9, 2020

What if nothing is an accident, not like divine hands manipulating marionette strings, but in the way that connections abound.

Just recently confronting the way hope blinds me to all kinds of warning signs. How we want to believe what we want to believe so badly we push evidence of the contrary to the background. Into the realm of things we concede, things we "know" in an abstract or intellectual way. Into the realm of someone else's job to act on. The professionalism of making a difference. Thinking that's for activists, educators, experts or attorneys. Thinking that supporting them is enough.

I no longer know what enough is and if I ever think I know again, I will hold myself up for examination.

Enough is a place to land, a ground to stop on. But what is needed here is not stopping. To not cease our learning and our looking, to not say, It feels too bad or makes me too tired.

What if nothing is an accident. What if threads of meaning tie it all together. What if we're being asked not only to look and acknowledge but to relinquish our own mythology.

To serve and protect cannot coexist where fraternity comes before justice.

Part of how these unjust systems have stayed in place so long has been under the guise of Freedom and Justice for All. We did it, white Americans want to believe.

Civil Rights achieved, like a level unlocked in this game decades ago. But it's like the criminalization of Black people and the new Jim Crow. We've changed the name and maybe the narrative but the impact is the same. New branding, same bullshit.

What if nothing is an accident. Not moving to Flatbush, not even nonsense like the bank closing my accounts. Not wider events beyond my own city streets. What if threads of meaning and purpose are there, just waiting to be connected and woven together.

Would we see the pattern enough to unravel it, enough to not create the same oppression under a new name?

Thursday, June 11, 2020

It began like this. The bed stripped of its top clothes for summer, a single white sheet that has never, ever been ironed. Lines and creases across its surface like the palm of a hand.

I wish there was someone here to read it.

It began like this. A blue journal and a blue pen, some ideas of things to do in the day. The future, still something opaque—a stranger I have not yet met.

Questions on a merry-go-round in my mind:

- What about belief and faith and trust?
- What about pragmatism and building a life that works?
- What if we think in shorter spans—four months, four years max?

I wish my friends could all live together in a great big house. I wish we could drive our expenses so far down we could do anything we want.

I've been trying to get back to the dorm ever since I left it. Four months. Four years.

It began like this. Mind drifting into the future fog then coming back to now. Stay here, long enough to finally take out the trash and fold the ever-present laundry. Long enough to empty the coat closet and find the summer shoes.

There was a relief in the beginning to let go of the future for a moment, to know it was too far from reach and too difficult to imagine.

But summer brings us back to fall. And how it is coming. What could happen then?

It began with a deep detachment from our future obsessions that let us return to the present and examine the past. A time to reflect, to witness, to set new things in motion.

The cat drapes across a greeting card from Steph and my still-closed laptop. My heart travels great distances on the inside, while my body is so often still.

It begins like this: kitty paws around my finger and cool air blowing in from the courtyard. A friend visiting tomorrow.

School projects wrapping up. A sleepy, indoor summer ahead and a trail of question marks pressed into the ground in front of me.

PM

I have a new habit now. When I climb out of my bath at night and wrap my towel around, I sit on the closed toilet seat lid, as if I can't make it all the way to standing.

I sit there, frozen, for so long.

As if inertia has tagged me into its game. I don't even know what I do there. Listen to the music? Read? Think?

I just know the bed feels too far to reach. A journey worthy of a carriage and a horse, maybe. A small travel case and documents.

It's a mistake, the sitting down just then. But I try to allow it. Who is waiting for me, anyway? And for what?

It's hard to sleep long when these summer days stretch deep into morning and evening. But I don't mind the light.

Tonight, in my bath towel sitting I thought, I am yearning for a work future the way some people ache for love.

Friday, June 12, 2020

Inspired by "finding your way to Bodieu" by Maya Stein

There are no instruction manuals and maps are useless here. News of the virus and the economy could just be a single word banner over the day: Uncertainty.

It's no use reaching back to moves you tried before. Facing the clean slate just as you are in this moment, not the last one, is the only way through.

There's something new you can see now, from this place. Maybe this is a sign the ground has shifted beneath you. It doesn't feel like forward motion, more like walking the wrong way on a moving walkway. More like the ground moving beneath while you've stepped your feet in an attempt to stay in place. There is no direction, really, just the feeling of turning to goo inside the chrysalis. The way so many things feel like complicity with the systems that are hurting us all.

These are thoughts I have on a Friday at one in the afternoon.

I'm not even sure there's a compass anymore, though maybe one will emerge.

Right now I'm deep in the undoing and in the being undone.

How do we move forward through such thick mist, through such unraveling?

Usually my work is about creation but so much uncreating in this season.

What if there was no map. What if I surrendered the future as an idea and returned to the day. When did I leave it?

(Again. Again. Always and again.)

Would today carry one into a month of tomorrows naturally, just as the sun marks days without my effort or strategy or plan.

Would the wisdom of my body instruct about the way to move through the day. Or could I let a day simply wash over me, the light shifting across the floor, my feet and my face.

Could I let a day happen to me, as a passenger. Could I close my eyes through a quiet stretch and rest.

Sunday, June 14, 2020

Today a handwritten card arrived from Caren, from England. It has artwork of a kitten on the cover who looks just like Linus.

Today time spent under a weighted blanket and eye pillow, listening to Tibetan bowls. Messages to a friend and worrying afterward that I was too sleepy/sloppy and didn't get my words right.

The Lost Feeling Days are vulnerable for me. Some days talking things through orders my heart, but on days like today I think I should have sat with the questions longer inside myself. I should have waited for an answer. The waiting means restless resting.

Today, messaging with Bella and dreaming of her garden.

I had actual dream dreams last night. In one, I needed my mom. She got on a flight and was here by morning. Somewhere deep inside I know this is who she is for me, whatever the circumstances are.

The second dream I can't remember.

I am playing always, always at the edges of myself.

The last years are hard to make sense of. They have largely been about falling into the net, but maybe I'm coming into a place I could weave one again for others to have, too.

You're not alone, I tell her. *Everything I make is saying this, again and again.*

Creative company. These are words I'm sitting with tonight. Creative company. Learning and community for artful journeys.

Maybe the answer falls out of one's mouth like a baby tooth from the mouth of a six year old. Wiggle, wiggle, feeling the sharp dig of something no longer in its proper place.

And then—

Out. Just as one bites into an apple, or a quiet tumble out onto the table's surface.

Maybe the answer falls out just like this. Maybe this is the quiet, humble beginning of what's next. What's ready? Maybe I am and maybe not. But the gap feels strange to my tongue.

Monday, June 15, 2020

It's Monday and this is what I know. A morning shower can be refreshing in the summer. Strange sensations move through my abdomen. Maybe it's my digestion or maybe it's the future I'm gestating rolling over, an elbow poking as it goes.

It's Monday, and this is what I know. It's possible I have some belief inside me yet. It's possible my magic is not all spent and maybe my lips could form the word "yes" one more time.

This is what I know—the world ahead is uncertain as it ever was, maybe even more so. But perhaps we could have each other as we go.

This is what I know. Tenderness is called for, and patience. And a sprinkle of stardust.

As always I'm interested in more than my own good idea. I'm interested in guidance. Some invisible help that will carry the parts outside my control.

I know it takes courage to hope but in this moment it seems I have precious little to lose, except time. And I have some of that to spare, so.

Maybe there is a summoning of my works and my powers into something useful. Maybe Francisco is right and the world is ready. Now there is just me, waiting to pull my offering into focus. It comes. It comes. It comes.

It's Monday and this is what I know. We are all changed by these times, unless we are asleep. We are slowed down eyes open finally listening and feeling all that living requires.

It's been like adjusting to a different heart gravity, even though our bodies are more at rest. It's the thing I've held at bay—the slow down. The stay in. The calendar open and no future to spend my mind in, just the surrender to the day.

This day. And may there be another one after. More slow living deep listening heart-learning days to come.

Please come.

Wednesday, June 17, 2020

Inspired by "Darkness is Asking to Be Loved" by Zenju Earthlyn Manuel

Make a river of it. The not knowing and the becoming. The tears of our heartbreaks and the things we must live without.

Make a river of the melodies that bubble over smooth rocks like a brook inside you. Feel it out play it out wash it all out. The way your little one cried for an hour the other night, their heart hurts and griefs spilling over. How you feel them. How you long to stitch their hurting places back together. But they will be their own medicine.

Come down on all fours and remember you don't know the ending of a day let alone a life.

Bring your gaze to the earth and her ancient rhythms. A fire, like its own kind of river at her core.

I never thought I'd say this but I am sometimes afraid. I think I could face anything as long as I had togetherness to shore me up or keep me upright. Togetherness like oxygen that keeps color in my cheeks.

I will try to hope and stay open, even though the world crumbles in my worst dreams and sometimes seems it really will be so.

There is always the need for each other, and I am surely not the only one.

Here I am, a river of worries and heart spilling sorrows.

This is my surrender—naming and feeling them all. This is the graveyard of my own losses I walk through now, laying in tree shade to listen and learn.

How I needed you then, I say.

How I carry you with me now.

Now it flows. Now my palms relinquish their grip and my cheeks cease their anxious smiling. Cheerfulness is not really ever the truth.

What is the truth, dear one. How you are still here. How nothing is wasted. How the future arrives in its own time and your only dance partner is today. The music plays.

Thursday, June 18, 2020

I don't know what to make of it. The way I stumble at small talk and sometimes fail at feeling out the lines.

The way a "new friend" feels like an oxymoron to me. I want to be already old friends, as soon as possible.

I only want to talk about the world as fireworks boom and glow against an overcast sky.

I want the stars to shine on my face just as much as I want the daylight sun.

I want to sit with the night now. I used to sleep through it.

To feel the subway rumble up through the ground, through bricks and stories like earth tremors we don't feel until they are pointed out to us.

And now I am slower than I used to be. And now I am still learning to listen. And now I will let the day move through me, instead of the other way around.

Here's what I really want to say. I am a swirl and a steadiness, both at once. I am stirred up and simmering and boiling over at times. That sizzle of the overflow hitting the stovetop, the smell of burning from the next room.

There is a frequency I am training my ear to hear. It sounds like not being able to hear myself in so many moments. Like static. But sometimes. Some. Times. I can feel it.

It makes me still and quiet but also clear. I crave clarity like fruit in summer, little appetite for words.

Maybe despairing of what I thought they might hold, now looking to stillness. But here is my pen, still moving, still learning to receive and to name the things.

Like how I want to bathe my kids in affection because my heart spills over for them. How I miss community and joy in my living space. How I dream of lighter days to come. Connectedness. Celebrations, big and small. Smiles. So many smiles and soft touches. Photographs and new paintings and memories. A window to the world that is never covered. A hearth warmth that flickers year round.

Something that feels like peace and freedom of a certain kind.

Sunday, June 21, 2020

What if it's all just one big story. Everything that happened before, what you remembered versus what you forgot and how you strung the pieces together. Everything you made it mean.

What if it's all just one big story, who loves us or doesn't and whether it's correct or enough. Whether we were worthy of it.

Whether it might come ever again.

It's hard to imagine tonight, like so many things. I feel like I understand so much more than I did before but I'm not sure I have any more words than I did before.

Or maybe I'm just afraid of them.

It's frightening, maybe, to know love, because of the way it shows where love isn't. Or what you thought was it but didn't know better.

Love needs something for a long run.

Tonight I'm weary from sun and heat and walking. From

talking with Maggie and the way I'm maybe pleasant company until maybe I'm not.

Tonight I'm reaching back to feel or remember something. I think it's love. How I'm trying to remember what it was like, even from my friends.

How Caren said the other night I'm one of her favorite people in the world and it made me cry.

I just would like to live with someone who is glad I'm alive in the world another day. I'm low on love like a person struggling for enough oxygen.

It could be a long pandemic.

I guess we'll see. The play for tonight is rest. Maybe an audiobook as I drift to sleep.

Each one, a way I'm either striving to be better or hoping to be reassured.

Monday, June 22, 2020

Let's get right to it. The way my oldest has such clear and good wisdom that this morning I think: Maybe I should be writing these down in a collection. *Breakfast with Amelia.*

How does she always know what I should do? Why is it always so hard to know for ourselves.

Work possibilities are stirring my curiosity this morning. My mind feels like a heavily populated aquarium. So many creatures swimming around, my eyes scarcely know where to go.

Maybe love isn't the only source for vitality and courage.

Maybe possibility works, too.

What is it I want to say? Actually, I know in my heart of hearts because they play like a chorus repeating after every verse.

I am always saying them.

I am always saying our stories matter. Our stories have the power to change others, the telling of them can heal us and help us find each other.

What I'm always and forever saying is: You're not alone.

Start right here. Start close in, as David Whyte says, and just see what might come after. Today I'll start with this, and another new idea will simmer in the background.

Maybe work is its own kind of love, its own field for seeing and being seen.

Maybe I can pour it all into the pot and give a big stir. Mix. Simmer. Take longer to finish than my impatience allows for.

But no rushing natural processes for artificial results.

I want the real thing, or nothing.

I don't mind giving up old stories for the truth. I want the truth like that rare moment you don't mind being naked, or draping yourself skin to skin.

The moment when you forget about clothes, or just don't need them anymore.

Tuesday, June 23, 2020

Not all nights are for sleeping. I haven't figured out exactly what inner workings are at play in the others, but my attempts to go back to sleep are usually the same. Warm toast, an audio program, and eventually as the sun rises again—surrender.

Two hours might be enough to get me through.

But it's a mystery—not just because a child and a kitty are creeping companions I'm configuring around—but also because I can feel other things at play.

Not all nights are for sleeping. Some are for unraveling old stories and learning new ones. Something driving or pushing forward in a way that demands our awakeness, even in the dark.

It is in so many ways this kind of night right now, even though the sun keeps lapping across the sky and our minds blend like thick porridge across the days.

There is much to dismantle and re-imagine. There are old mythologies that kept harsh realities at bay.

Nights like this demand we let the old myths go and learn, not by rote but by turning around to look straight on at how we got here. To face our romanticism or idealism and the way they were just a cover. The way ignorance allows and conspires with violence.

Not all nights are for sleeping. Mostly there is no revelation or reward waiting like an easy exchange for lost slumber.

There is only the living pushing its way through whatever each day and night holds—the short ones and the ones that last months or years.

Wednesday, June 24, 2020

Let's take inventory:

1. Books started but not finished.
2. Friends I miss, and
3. laughter. The big belly, cheek-bursting variety. Being able to reach absurdity through solemnity.
4. Tenderness. In every form and gesture I've ever known it.
5. This way of letting myself go that feels like head thrown back and hands released and hanging by my side.
6. The times I've believed in magic or felt it draw near, like a ballet rehearsal by a summer fountain and a tutu sprinkled with twinkle lights.
7. "The world is here for you, for this moment," they seemed to whisper.
8. My body vibrant and vital, my passion streaming through creative channels and not just rage.
9. The impulse that shot me straight out of bed in the morning, no matter how early it came.
10. Looking in a mirror with recognition.
11. Ocean waves and the call back thundering in my chest.
12. Prairie.
13. Sky.
14. My mother's cheek against mine.
15. Food that makes my mouth grateful to be alive.
16. The year that tears came every day. They had somewhere to go, then.
17. Feeling lost and then finding myself again. How the finding was so sweet.

18. The future as something to look forward to.
19. Not wondering if any color is left in my cheeks because I felt it coursing through.
20. The fleeting feeling, in red shoes stepping onto a stage, of being made for a moment.
21. Times when beauty sustained, like something that could be ingested and made part of me.
22. Headstones and graves reminding me I'm still this side of Earth's surface.
23. Knowing what to do next.
24. Falling into the net. Being caught.
25. Being held. Being held. Being held.

Friday, June 26, 2020

This is the journey. No maps, no footsteps to follow. A small lantern, if you're lucky. A clue pointing the next foot forward but no farther.

This is the journey—to sit in the directionless not knowing. To wait. To surrender oneself to the great unraveling of who we once knew ourselves to be so there's an opening for who we're becoming to step through.

Nothing fits in the meantime. One's clothes feel all wrong, maybe this soft belly feels foreign and the name we took now chafes like an old rope rubbing the wrists.

This is the journey—keeping oneself alive on some backpack

snacks—really just rudimentary moves like food, sleep, sun and water—until clarity comes and returns your vitality with it. Until you come roaring back to life with passion and purpose and a color in your cheeks very much like falling in love.

This too is the journey—leaving old companions back in their seasons, even though you long to reach them. Loving is certainly also letting go, or learning to match those who now only wish to touch you lightly, or not at all.

It's important to know what season you're in and keep orienting yourself. This is the ground you stand on. These are the travelers at your side.

This is the waiting. The long belly of the night that threatens to last forever.

Waking will come, some day. So you might as well rest up so you'll be ready.

The real work reveals itself in its own time, it's not at your beck and call. You are the servant here, not the master. And new works can't be made by old selves.

The waiting is the becoming. The soul checked into the garage, or beating out a faint pulse on life support.

These cheeks, now gray and heavy, will lift again. These lips will part
and they will know
what to say.

Saturday, June 27, 2020

She reminds me that listening to Dinah Washington makes me feel better and she's right.

I forget sometimes, after another turntable died. The records I got for Christmas never even got played.

At least three broken turntables, waiting to be taken out to some more permanent resting place after the pandemic.

My breath catches on a hook inside my throat when I see them and remember all the songs that go unplayed now.

How five unplayable players over these last many years feel like a metaphor for other things.

All I ever wanted was to hear the music.

But now we have digital and bluetooth earbuds and I'll remember to pull up Dinah tonight. She'll sing about love, which I'm sometimes not in the mood for.

But she'll also sing about Manhattan and remind me what the city is like when we get to live out in it.

When we talk about this time will we remember our worlds got so small, pulled in close inside our physical walls and maybe a grocery store down the street.

Will we remember how it was hard to keep holding our heads up after a while? Or how we all hit the F A D E at different times?

Would I feel differently inside other walls, is the mystery. With other singers in my ears?

Or is it just the grief and sorrow and mourning and rage about all that is wrong seeping in. Is it just part of having a heart for feeling and ears for hearing.

Tonight I can hardly hold up my head and my pen to write. Something takes me. A great inner work, or a small giving up—it's hard to say.

Tomorrow I will leave and see a friend. She'll bring a bunch of lavender and I'll dream of a trip with her up north to stay by a lake.

What music will play then? Please let something make me dance soon.

Monday, June 29, 2020

For the activists camping out at City Hall, with their laundry and garden stations, and a pop-up library for Black lives. Huddled under tree shade with a Wifi setup rigged on a post nearby.

For the Black educators in District 3 who have lost their jobs. For other city employees who will soon follow.

For everyone who is hungry tonight.

For fireworks at three am and a mayor who lost his way.

For my kids and color-coded eyeshadow with new themes every day.

For this blue notebook my mother sent when she was so far away but wanted me to feel loved.

For cold Oatly mochas and drowsy afternoons. For protests and police attacking on the anniversary of Pride.

For everyone who is afraid and those who don't know enough to be.

For family members.

For afternoon siestas not even caffeine can touch. For incremental journeys, like the videos of snails my friend Alisha keeps sharing.

All forward movement counts.

All forward movement counts.

For the way we long for rest but then resist when it finally arrives. For the way we feel undeserving of it, even though so little in this moment is a choice. For piano notes falling like rain drops, the big kind one easily tracks down a windshield between the wipers.

For surprising companions for this strange season, and the way a blue pen and stacks of notebooks can be a pathway we needed.

For us and the way we go on, into uncertainty and imperfection. For the ways we are brave enough to learn and change.

New futures from new selves. A resilience we can build now, like a muscle, if we haven't before.

Time, like an accordion, stretching and collapsing to an unknown melody.

We didn't fancy ourselves dancers before but this song is for all of us. We tap a foot, stand up and step in, not knowing where we are or what time it is,

but not caring, either.

Part 2

I write because I was quiet for so long. I learned young that so many things were not to be asked about or spoken of, and I wanted to follow the rules even if I didn't understand them.

I write because what we witness matters. Because reality gains permanence when we name it.

I write so I will not be a stranger to myself.

I write because my heart is broken and its soft center needs somewhere to flow.

I write because this life was entrusted to me. It's a duty to pay attention and to say the things.

Even the ones I learned not to say. Especially those.

I want to ask myself some questions. Like, What does any of it matter in the end?

It isn't the words, my aunt told me this morning, it's the way they made you feel.

I write because the pen sometimes feels like my only weapon, only tool. My only recourse.

You can't change the story, a friend told me once.

But you can tell it.

To be a namer, a witness, a keeper of stories not as a collection of facts but as an energy that passes through and alters us.

The stories that change us as we tell them, and as we hear them.

This is what I am here for.

It means climbing up onto the story altar again and again. To be made new as it forms inside my organs, inside my ribs.

It means rising, weak in body but unrelenting in heart.

It means taking my place. On stage. Online. Behind a camera or on a big screen.

It means risking everything for the truth and trusting love—a very real and true kind—to still await me on the other side.

I'm coming. We will be made new, together.

Tuesday, June 30, 2020

I want a large poster framed at the foot of my bed, titled:
How to Keep Going.

I want gorgeous typography and clever design to arrange wisdom in easy phrases I repeat like mantras and imagine tattooed on my arm.

How to keep going, it would tell me every morning. Don't stop, it might say. Don't give up.

Rest when you need to. When your optimism wanes, try sleep first, and if that doesn't work try yelling your rage in the streets.

Forget imagining the future or planning for it and stomp your feet firmly in the ground of today.

Remember the children are watching and find the best inside of you for them.

Some days I would hate the words. They would feel weak and naive, like a band aid after a car crash.

No, honestly, I would say, as if it were a conversation in real time.

How to not lose heart. How to not spend ourselves to the bottom of the bottom. How to refill in a real way.

How to find the core of oneself that does not rise and fall but is solid, like iron.

How to burn every unnecessary part away and get down to all that ever mattered.

What we must do and stand for as long as breath enters us. This heart beating. These lungs breathing.

As long as they do.

As far as the sound of this life travels.
Let it be heard. Let it be felt.

July 2020

Wednesday, July 1, 2020

I didn't think I would write about it but I'm feeling hunger right now. Every time the sensation comes I feel it even more internally than in my organs.

Like not only my body is in need of nourishment and sustenance.

What is it that I crave. Ocean waves for sure. The feeling of stripping away every garment with abandon, as if it's the only way we were ever meant to be.

Horns saying it better with the breath passing through them than words ever can.

Something like a bed and pillow and soft white sheets, except for my spirit.

Surrendering to love. Laying down my attempts to predict or control and admitting defeat.

The belief that something greater carries or holds us. Love like a cosmic force, conspiring inside the universe of a body to lift one's head.

Understanding force and power and how they fit into the scheme of things.

Having my chin lifted upward.

Hearing the heartbeat of another.

Losing myself in pleasure. Falling into time like a black hole. Transcending every role and label.

The way stillness feels like the purest form of prayer.

Make me new, if words could be pebbles falling from lips on an altar.

Hearts I could drop anchor into and locate myself with.

The sonar ping that bounces back with a chorus of Not Alone Down Here. In the good way.

The way whale songs change as they travel across oceans and around continents. And yet the way they sing on.

Friday, July 3, 2020

I'm thinking of generational stories and what gets embedded in either our DNA or culture.

It all goes back to the farm, we sometimes say, my aunt and I, drinking coffee on the screened porch or riding in the car through tree-lined curves.

Maybe the biologist in her thinks of the animal kingdom, and the way one generation can learn to avoid a poisonous plant and pass the knowledge down inside its genetic code.

What's in our code, I wonder. Where did we learn to be afraid and does it come through our bodies and not just our minds?

It's in the way we think about money, always wanting to store up in case of lost crops or bad weather. We brace for calamity.

Our biology is older than credit cards.

Is it also in the way we view work and rest? No day is entirely a holiday or a day of mourning when the cow needs to be milked. Living off the land meant work that did not wait.

Except in winter. Every time my body heads into deep hibernation I wonder if I am still on the old schedule. The sleep-soon-after-sundown one when there was not much to do after dark.

But I wonder now about what came before even that. Whose land we settled on and what was the true story of what happened to them. Now I wonder about how taking is in our inheritance, too.

I wonder about survival and safety and how every generation gives us space to learn a new way.

But it's the unconscious ways that are most harmful, that most need my eyes. All that is old in me. Young brides, sisterhood over wifedom.

A pink house in a town called Kanorado where the bath water is soft like silk on your skin. Where children are scarce and those we visit feel old. Where Dairy Queen serves burgers with mustard and my great-grandad's gas tank is underneath his license plate.

Rocking chairs and crossword puzzles and a dead bird under a tree outside.

Grandma Winoma's picnic and how living 100 years makes a body so small, whittled away by all we've seen and survived. The way we try and catch the stories and archive them and how I might wish I had, too.

My prairie-born grandfather and the way he still needs to lay his eyes on the sky.

The sky the sky the sky.

Horizons on every side and ourselves old and tired in the dust, even when we are still so young.

Sunday, July 5, 2020

I don't want to tell you that I'm barely holding onto my heartbeat over here. I don't want to say that even now I can't hold up my head without a hand or a wall to support it.

I don't ever want to say that it was hard, this time, or how completely I unraveled.

I don't want to talk about how many times I've compared myself to Humpty Dumpty because it might reveal a penchant for falling apart.

I'd rather pass lightly always, over the parts that crumble me under their heavy heel. I use phrases like, "It's fine", or "I'm fine" like Wonder Woman bracelets—a deflection on each wrist.

I'm fine, I say in the daydreams. It's fine. It happens. Shrug. Look anywhere else but someone's face. Pandemics. Divorce.

Whatever. Like a flip that brushes long hair behind me—over my shoulder and out of sight. Unworthy of even a conscious gesture, just this absent-minded toss to reside outside my view.

Behind me, like it's all no big deal. That's life, I might say, and launch into the next topic to show there's nothing to say here.

Is there nothing to say, really?

I don't want to say that fantasy sometimes tugs at my toes. Or that reality is inhospitable and doesn't notice if I leave anyway.

I don't want to say that experiencing love illuminates the places it's missing. I want to say I've forgotten everything that makes me grieve

and I want to mean it.

I don't want to confess that I am unmoored and not myself, my body limp and inanimate.

I don't want to need anyone. I don't want to need love, like
a plant needs sun. I want to will myself back to life. I want to
believe I can do anything that's required.

I want to believe a future waits for me but it all tends to feel
like trading one struggle or hardship or sorrow for the next one
again and again on repeat.

I don't want to say I'm afraid I don't mend right, this time.
Like a bone not set right but in my heart. I don't want to feel
discarded or rejected over and over. I think a small shrug is so
useful for this.

"It is what it is."

"Life is a coin toss."

There would just be me, too strong and too cool to be bothered
with heartbreak or longing.

Dust off the knees.

Back on the bike.

Cry when you get home but not out here. Not where it can be
seen.

Nurse the wounds quietly, and later trace the scabs and scars.
That one doesn't leave, I don't want to say.

A strange limp left in my loving, but all I would say about it is:
I'm fine.

Tuesday, July 7, 2020

I'd rather not say anything about love right now. I'd rather not hear about it or sing about it. If I'm honest I'd rather not forecast its presence or its absence into my future.

Some piece of it I've always felt excluded from—like a nun from my own kind of order. The "I was a nun in a former life" kind, or "I would have been one if my branch of religion had them" kind.

The "I'll be a nun anyway even though I long ago left the religion behind" kind.

"Maybe in my next life," I told a friend once about this romantic variety of love.

She paused before saying in a quiet voice, "What if we only get the one?"

Maybe I'm actually afraid of my hunger for intimacy—the breadth and depth of it—and I doubt any one love's ability to satisfy.

But maybe I've never known what I haven't known.

Maybe every love is a resignation in the end. I receive these things and choose to live without others.

Sometimes we're quite far down the road before we realize we negotiated poorly. Lived with things we couldn't live with or lived without ones we couldn't actually live without.

A heavy enough thought that it sends me staring into the middle distance.

Maybe they all feel the same in the beginning. Or maybe it's about being too young to know what our negotiables and non-negotiables are yet.

Maybe something sweet will find me some day, but I cannot wait until then to resurrect myself and keep going.

Today we cleaned the apartment and it feels like I will make it after all. The cleared tabletops say, "You will not drown in these sorrows." The washing machine is a symbol of fresh starts, dryer balls roll through new beginnings.

I'm thinking of damsels in distress and tragic figures and the romanticism of being lost in our heartbreak forever.

What small stories these are. What others can be told.

That parting could be hopeful, not because it clears space for someone else but because it chooses ourselves.

Because it learns the line and draws it, not just in sand but in fresh concrete.

This is what I will live with now, and what I won't live without. This is the territory of my own country. I welcome kindred visitors and native speakers but keeping the borders clearly marked and enforced is mine, all mine.

I am built for love, in whatever form it comes. I am its torch bearer. At its service, now and ever.

Wednesday, July 8, 2020

Summer is so hot in Brooklyn that I sleep with only a single sheet. It makes for a wrinkled top cover, and near the foot of the bed is a lump where I rolled up a towel because when I sleep on my stomach it's nice to drape my ankles over it.

I was looking at the bump this morning—my eyes were resting on it—when I told my therapist that I'm always trying to find the thing under the thing. I see its outline—I know something is there, even if someone else's eyes might pass right over it—and I'm just trying to figure out, all the time, how to lift the sheet.

Like this time I had a babysitter—a rare occurrence in my very early childhood—who fell asleep on the couch. I remember lifting up her sweater, curious to see her bra underneath and feeling shocked to be met with a bare breast instead.

I knew even then, this was a trespass. Wrinkled summer sheets and knit sweaters should stay in place.

No peeking.

What is the thing under the thing?

Last night I thought about projects I've made in recent years and why I made them. There are always reasons, and never only the ones we let ourselves admit and boast about in marketing posts and trailers.

But the shadow reasons we hardly even tell ourselves. I was grossed out last night when I saw it—but I have wanted to show how I am loved.

Like a magician performing sleight-of-hand—if you see that I am loved here perhaps you won't see the other part.

The part I'm afraid to show is how I haven't been loved in that way by the person who was supposed to be my person. And that any of the things I've told myself might be true. That I'm too much for people, that people like me at first but then it wears off. After they say "I do", after sex, after life transitions from fantasy into domesticity. Or worst of all that I'm hard to love, or simply unlovable.

So I keep thrusting into the world these other proofs: Yes, but *these people* know me and *these people* love me so that must count for something.

The oldest story, the one that goes back to the beginning—not wanting to be a mistake. Even now, looking back through all those relationships and wondering if they regret me now.

Wondering if it's my fate to always want more than can be given.

To be a sojourner, plumbing the depths. Hitting the bottom of one well and continually moving with my water stick back out onto the land.

Friday, July 10, 2020

We write alone. Sometimes it feels like death to me this way. I resist the aloneness of it, like a child not wanting to look under the bed after dark or walk into the abandoned house in the woods without a friend. I always want the way a good companion makes me feel more brave. I'm always rigging ways for them to poke into the shadow places with me.

Inside I am still six years old. And jumpy, with a high-pitched little scream that escapes with the slightest provocation.

I am a truth-teller who is constantly trying to skirt around the truth. Wanting partial credit for getting close.

It is sadly an all or nothing game. The story can ring true or the alternative, in its absence, is to ring false.

There is something around devotion I come back to. Something I don't want to talk about. How I could lose devotion to a faith and a husband could lose devotion to me. How I was taught that faith was often a sacrifice, not a feeling, and that the same might also be true of love.

Where does devotion get a person in the end?

What path is there, ever, to follow except our own?

It takes something to unpack the part that was taught to worship and the one taught to glorify martyrdom in all its forms.

I still catch myself latching onto new gods.

Or looking for someone greater to love than myself. But loving myself is the only thing that gets me out of this strange cycle. It's the single rope hanging down this dark hole.

Now there is just building the strength and stamina to climb it. And knowing it takes time and many attempts but maybe I will get there in the end.

One try and another. The dinner dishes and finding a new bank. Even now my mind wanders.

What do I really want to say. I hear a new direction and I am following where it leads. That is all for now.

That is everything.

Sunday, July 12, 2020

I am deep in missing today. So deep that I'm running late, letting the day pass me by as I look at the notes populating my wall. I miss the story mechanics so hard I can hardly breathe. I can hardly trust myself to get there without them.

Feeling alone in the story garage. I have my friends and am trusting I have the correct people for this season but I miss the listening of the last seasons.

This morning I woke from a dream I had a chance to score a film when my feet hit something wet in the sheets. So. Much. Cat vomit. I am trying to not make it a metaphor for anything. Sometimes messes happen and all there is to do is clean them up.

Why do I feel like crying? Was it hearing Mike Birbiglia and Ira Glass on a podcast this morning and the way it made me miss old friends? I think it was Ira's listening. His ear for where it worked and where it didn't.

I am trying to make new connections for myself now but it doesn't always work. Maggie cancelled our time today because she needs to work. I swing so quickly from lit up and in the flow to I can't hold up my head.

Who will be my people in this season? Who are they already and will I let myself land with them? How will I battle through my aloneness and in this particular time, how will we all?

Yesterday I could hold myself steady for a few minutes. I'd like to find that feeling and expand it. Five minutes a day, then maybe ten. Could I make it to five hours? Or is that too much to ask for. It is too close to faith for my comfort. Too solitary for my heart. I need to pull someone into the story circle soon, unless it's a crutch I'm meant to walk without. All I know today is I'm limping through and leaning my head against the wall.

Monday, July 13, 2020

I think the time has come. To stop pretending or exaggerating. No need for damsels here.

The time has come for being sturdy and strong and well and deserving of love and care anyway. The time has come for eyes closed, scenes arriving like reflections in a pool just after waking.

The time has come for gentle twists and my body stretched out long on the floor, then up and reaching for an invisible sky.

The time has come for grape KoolAid and unparenting and a moisturizer that's even creamier than I think I need. It's time to become, quietly here in my haven, but every now and then to say hello. It's time to take the medicine and finally, finally even out.

It's time to let it be okay, however it's gone and however we got here. It's okay to stop blaming and call it like a doctor declaring time of death. No story needed. Just a heartbeat that stopped.

It's time now to greet the day without casting my eyes ahead to other days the whole time. It's probably time for four bean salad and painting next to my children on their island of a bed.

It's time to grow bored of tragedy and to fall in love with playfulness. To let the light be the light. To realize dread doesn't serve anyone. To choose myself and not worry if I'm chosen by anyone else or not. To be a fellow traveler and adventurer.

It's time to rethink forward motion and embrace a new ethic that's something more like dancing with the day. At least for now. Soft light through thin curtains and story cards every now and then tumbling off the wall.

What can we do when our plans for the future disappear like a math sum being wiped from a chalkboard? What can we do when even the distance that separated us before grows farther?

When all our ways of attempting "progress" are taken off the table and something called survival left in its place.

What can we do but turn back to the past with yearning. The last time cool air blew our hair as it came off the water. The last time we were tenderly held. A time we tasted our mother's food.

I still think of ribs rising and falling when I can't fall asleep. I think about the stars in Ohio and the first shower after returning to this country. Wild turkeys in a New England field early in the morning. The way my grandmother looks right after she wakes up.

I've always loved hands, and voices close enough to sound like a storm in my ear. I held cameras and moved in all kinds of ways to get the shot right. I sat in dark anonymous rooms, sometimes stepping briefly into a spotlight and then back into the shadows again.

I pushed little ones in swings and danced in the kitchen with our aprons on. I pulled grass blades one by one and ran my finger along their length. I flew to cities sight unseen. I drank tea in the Village among spirits and ghosts.

I wandered, just as I do now. Ending up in the same places, whether by a skyline or a lake, or in a field of headstones and graves.

I am always searching, but somehow I am never lost.

Only weary or heart worn. Only resting and gathering. I am that invisible sky—clear then overcast, summoning my substance and falling, lightly or in thick bucket pours back to the ground.

Tuesday, July 14, 2020

Even after all this time, I still have days that feel like pudding. Full but somehow shapeless with no visible result to show by the end. "I really am working," I catch myself saying to my kids or friends, none of whom are asking or implying otherwise.

My work so often looks like Not Work that I often can't shake off the self-consciousness. Yes, I'm watching another movie, but not like other people do. I'm studying it and researching as I write a new story into this complex shape. So many justifications for critics who only reside in my mind.

I just did my yoga practice and it is that drowsy hot time before dinner when I yawn in a way that makes tears fill and sting my eyes.

No one wants to think about dinner. To weigh options and choose one, to go to the store and carry ingredients up four flights. No one wants to turn on the oven or boil water into our already humid air.

It's a night that makes me remember this one time my dad made chocolate shakes for dinner with vanilla ice milk and Hershey's chocolate syrup and served them alongside omelettes.

That night felt like magic. Maybe it's a milkshakes for dinner night here too.

But what do I really want to tell you and say. My body is so tired from the smallest exertion but I'm getting stronger every day, I tell myself.

I am getting stronger every day. Every meal and good night of sleep. Every conversation with a friend. I am having ideas again. My mind is hearing and weaving the story while I sleep. I want to say don't lose heart yet, to myself. Keep going, not in that Keep Believing! kind of way but just the quiet steady way that sees the sweetness along the path. Don't lose heart and keep feeding your body and mind because you are churning now. You're onto something, and it will come.

Even the fatigue at the end of a day or a practice can be its own kind of relief, the body wrapping itself in a soft blanket of lowered output and the thing in you that loves to grip the steering wheel dropping to surrender instead.

Here I was, alive in this day. Fading now is the light that fell on me. Nothing was special to an outside observer, but this day and I, we danced.

Wednesday, July 15, 2020

First line from "Rebus" by Jane Hirshfield

You work with what you are given. Stiff pages, wider than you're accustomed to. Heart aching headlines and leg muscles like limp spaghetti noodles from yesterday's movements. Dirty hair and a mind not interested in unlocking the answers today.

I will watch another movie tonight, that has been nourishing. Something in me gathering, watching. Feeling the effect of this camera placement or that storytelling device.

In my fantasy it arrives all at once and fully-formed, but was it just earlier today I read about love? And how it does not truly arrive in an instant but requires time to become. Our storytelling is often too impatient for this. Hurry it along, we say, and tell us how it ends.

As if the ending tells you anything at all.

What I most love is the incremental moment, the small gesture and quiet thoughtfulness, again and again like layers. Each one an echo of I love you and together a small chorus.

I am for you, the layers harmonize as they rise in melody.

I am for you.

It feels like an invisible interior space we cohabit. Here is where we meet. Where we deliver our Good Mornings and Good Nights.

It becomes a house, love does, not just a feeling but a world we walk together. Rugs woven out of shared places and memories hung in a row on the wall. A candle lit for every hard question we were brave enough to answer truly.

Togetherness is a shared space, a co-created world. So of course a story would emerge slowly, like love.

Or at least the difficult ones would.

Slowly like a woman packing her possessions for a move. Holding each glass and plate gingerly as she wraps them in paper. This is looking at one's life. But the story is more like

unpacking into a new space. Where will the blue jam jar live now?
Maybe in this space it becomes a flower vase in a window sill.
Everything rearranged into a new place. Some pieces breaking
in transit, other new things needed for the arrival space to work.
Unwrapping. Looking around. Waiting.

Thursday, July 16, 2020

Every time I dive back into the story forming on my wall I feel
like I should tell someone first.

"I'm going in."

As if I'm journeying off the grid, out of reach. Or, like I'm
entering a haunted house alone and I need a rope tied around my
waist so if I die of fright my body could still be recovered.

What am I afraid of, really?

I'm afraid because it hurts to confront my past and the belief
systems that harmed me. I'm afraid because it's sad. Because I lost
so much in the end.

I'm afraid for all the reasons I've hesitated to tell it. Not
wanting to hurt anyone or "take" anything "down". I don't want
it to be a giant bomb. Just the small ones that one friend used to
say I sweetly strapped around my students' waists, to go off in
quiet ways even after they left me.

Just a small, quiet bomb—not to destroy anything but to shift
the way we think or see things. Like when they want to move a
river—don't they use dynamite or explosives for this?

I am trying to build a quiet bomb. A palatable and agreeable one it's impossible to argue with.

You either let it change you, or you don't.

Still trying to get to the thing I most want to say.

It's something like: Nothing kept its promise.

My character needs to have this moment. A place to have it and someone to hear her.

The question is, what do we do when it all falls apart?

I think we are broken, for a minute. The blast hits and it needs to reverberate through us and leave us a little dazed before we can pick up, reorient, and keep going.

I think this character stays in bed and almost doesn't graduate.

But in thinking of something to write for her final piece she does what I'm doing now—taking the pain and pulling it back out like a magician's string of scarves. Transformed into something new.

> *We sacrifice so much for being told or offered The Way. The right way to live, the right work to do, the right way to love. We give up so much of ourselves slowly, incrementally, because trying to fit into someone else's formula feels less frightening than facing our own future without one. If God is responsible for the outcome, we don't have to be.*
>
> *But outside answers haven't gotten me very far. They didn't even get me to graduation.*
>
> *Maybe it can be a gift, to find out sooner than later that no matter what's ahead, the path is mine to forge. There isn't one way for everyone, we are too varied for that. We were never lost, trapped or dangerous.*
>
> *We are glorious and brave, even though I can't always feel it.*
>
> *I'll keep going, just the same.*

Something like that might do it.

Friday, July 17, 2020

I was taught to tell the truth, but not to say things that would make anyone look bad or hurt anyone's feelings. Tell *some* truths, they meant.

Others are best held close to the chest like cards you never lay down on the table. Some can be said in a coded language, maybe, hidden or disguised.

Protect our reputation. Guard our feelings. Make us look good.

But there is no healing without setting the bones straight, without acknowledging sickness or infection.

I'm looking deep in every corner of memory. I am moving my body on the yoga mat, shaking things loose from my joints. Keep moving, I say to the chemicals released by all the feelings. You may pass through but you may not stay. This body is not a stress hormone hotel.

Tell the story, the lunge says, arms lifting up, then back, chest opening and lifting to the sky. Get it out, however you must. Braid it into fiction, put a mustache on it, or a wide brimmed floppy hat for disguise.

But get it out get it out get it out.

These fractured places realign and there will be no limp left in your loving going forward.

Get it out. The parts that make you laugh or sad or angry. The parts that felt like tragedy so you can get to the part on the other side that feels like hope.

My bracelet from Steph says, "I can't withstand the storm? I AM the storm."

I am the author of the narrative. I am the teller of this tale, and even though I will tell it in many changing ways over the years, it doesn't need to stop me from telling it this way now.

Write the poem, the screenplay, the journal entry. Take the beyond words and translate it into language. It doesn't fit exactly, we know, but it can't stay inside.

Move through, story, and move on. So I can, too.

So I will.

Saturday, July 18, 2020

I left with no purpose or destination, only because I needed to walk off the day in the last of its light.

Yes, I told the air, let's shrug it off like a cold damp robe and climb into something soft and warm.

And I saw life on my streets, like I always do. I'm the only one who stops to watch fireflies and I likely look disoriented to everyone passing by.

I still can't get over the magic of fireflies.

It's warm enough that neighbors gather on front steps, or talk on the phone from the stoop. I found a thrift store I didn't know was there when I turned down a different street than usual.

Will I remember this as the summer I spent so many nights on the roof, watching the Empire State Building and peering out over the trees? Will I remember craving my eyes to take in sky? Here you are right now, the earth says. Nowhere else but here.

I gather up all my presence for the right here-ness. I come back from daydreams and longings and I land back here at my desk, remembering I didn't do yoga today but I walked and climbed the stairs a couple times.

What does a heart really need in the end? A quiet desk, a blank page, a wide expanse of sky. My children, to kiss and hold tightly to my chest.

For the first time today I saw my parents over Zoom. It's different seeing them laugh than just hearing them over the phone. The way my dad's eyes crinkle at the corners, and his head throws back when he's amused by my mom. Showing them my home here in Brooklyn and seeing the new projects at theirs.

We talked so long, it was easy to forget we weren't actually together—I guess because we were. We really were, and it was so sweet.

I don't know what I need tonight before sleep finds me but I am dreaming in these pre-slumber moments. I shrug off the present, just for a little while, and imagine some sweet somethings to come.

Dear dream land, are you listening? Please let there always be sky.

.... Sunday, July 19, 2020

PM

"I guess we start again from here." - Anne Carmack, who has the loveliest name ever

From rumpled bed sheets that didn't get washed today and a face still slick with night cream.

From a body that craves sleep but often struggles to find it. Last night longing was a physical ache I tried everything to take my mind from. I finished a novel at 3:10 am.

My insomnia snack is gluten free toast with "butter" but we are all out of bread.

It felt in the early morning hours like something that should flash on the screen like a lower center title announcing The State of Things in This Scene:

All Out of Bread

Or we could start tomorrow, in the brighter eyes of morning. Tomorrow I will make it to the mat, weary or not.

(Please let tonight's sleep be magic.)

Or maybe we are always starting here and now.

How will I rock myself to sleep tonight? My eyelids are heavy but it doesn't always stop my mind.

Let's start here. Hair freshly detangled by Lucy's hands, Lucy who lives and sleeps in their room as if it's their own cocoon. Lucy, whose combing is gentle but firm.

Let's start here with the President's latest rambling and unmarked federal police escalating in Portland. Let's start with the ginger pineapple drink from Lips Café and officers posting up on my street without masks.

Here. So tired tonight my eyes water. In this bed where I'm coming up short on sleep too many nights.

The future a Yahtzee cup and each of us dice inside. Where will the next play send us? No one knows.

But today I sat in the courtyard and watched flies. I craved nature but had to take just small tastes.

Dear future, I am dreaming you into shape. I am closing my eyes now.

Monday, July 20, 2020

I have a tendency to think I'm doing it wrong. Anything. Everything.

This morning I watered some of the plants I missed this weekend. Two of the pots in my room have Chinese money trees, their trunks carefully shaped and braided together, held together with the kind of twist ties that keep bags of store-bought bread closed. My trees have new growth though, and I thought maybe I should gather these into a twist, too.

But when I tried I felt one fledgling branch give just a little too much at the base, and I stopped. All I could think of was seeing Black men's shoulders dislocated as police handcuffed them with force.

Sometimes I think I don't write enough details in these pages but maybe it's a mercy.

The hardship and heartbreak of the last years especially have kept me away from the page too long. What I wouldn't give to have carefully recorded accounts of the last year. I've tried piecing it together again in retrospect but it's not the same.

I don't want to be afraid to write the truth ever again. Too much of my own story has already been lost to a natural (and perhaps blissful) forgetfulness.

I don't want our collective memory to be lost the same way.

So I'll let them keep showing up here—the hard and heartbreaking parts—and worry about them later.

I want words and stories to spill out of me, uninhibited. I've been thinking of people who achieve this state of low resistance with substances and how there must be a way for me to get there through surrender.

Everyone wants a happy ending but I'm reminded watching films of others, of just how much struggle and discomfort are needed for us to open, awaken or transform. How the ending doesn't feel like a satisfying payoff unless it really took something to get there.

Am I shying away? I wondered yesterday. I know I have a tendency to do this. Is the truth even harder or more painful than I'm letting on? I wonder how far I have to go, how far is far enough. I am not bloodthirsty and I have little appetite for dark sides so I don't care to say any more than I need to.

It's the way I would tell you the story of watering my tree, but leaving out how my stomach turned at the memory of injured bodies. What's the whole truth, I'm asking today. And what am I willing to say.

✶   ✶   ✶

I have a blue-gray kitty laying on a sheepskin rug and plant leaves dancing to the beat of a ceiling fan. I have story cards papering my wall and a small stack of notebooks filling up. I have extra blueberries and granola begging for another cup of coffee to wash them down.

It feels like I should send a light flare soon but I'm still in the deep. Sometimes I can make myself say something, like diligently chewing and swallowing even though one's appetite is gone.

Still here. It looks like stillness on the outside but inside I am simmering and swirling and just hoping you wait for me. I can't get to the depth without giving myself a break from the surface.

I am finding the songs that unlock my mind like keys. I am communing with memories and ghosts and making sure the teens wake by noon. I am at my desk, on the mat, looking out from the rooftop and waving at neighbors on our streets.

I am reading the news and watching what feels like a house of cards collapsing in slow motion.

I am riding the waves of energy and humidity. I am hot and cold all night in a love/hate dance with air conditioning.

The words of friends keep me afloat and I gather my own words to be a small raft for someone else.

That's how generosity works.

All things considered, I'm a miracle right now but it looks like being an ordinary person whose weekly chores feel like they were just done yesterday, not eight days ago. It looks a lot like being a mom (or sometimes, a maid) but I'm deep-sea diving in all my in-betweens. I'm finding good things down there.

Tuesday, July 21, 2020

This is how the words come on a summer morning. They shake a little loose on Martense street, softened by the appearance of two toddler-sized chairs in the courtyard. They spill into a voice message to a friend.

They ramble a bit down this block and then turn the corner to stay in the shade. They get lighter things out of the way first, or noisier ones. The larger ones wait for the spot in the cemetery under the shade of a big tree.

Here the mask can come off. Here are reminders to not waste time thinking our time here is endless. Here is my own little refuge, out of earshot of strangers and in the company of birds.

The words think they want a song but quickly they are spilling out again, to other friends and another one still. My generous listeners who know I often can't get the answers out of me any other way.

The words keep coming as I wave to neighbors and as we dance around each other on the sidewalk, sneaking out Good Mornings between ideas. I must look like a spectacle.

But the words love a walk, they won't argue with a cool shower after and they quiet down on the mat.

They love blue ink more than black and spaces that don't cramp their style. They don't have much reason to be, outside the listening, so the listening matters a lot.

I wonder if the people who study bird calls ever figured out what any of the melodies mean. Certainly some signal danger and others mating, or something to do with food.

Also, whales. I'm thinking of them again this morning because the pandemic has created quieter waters for them to swim in and a better chance for those listening for whales to hear them. What do the whales have to say in this time?

I am ready to begin soon, making space for reflection and listening. A quiet space with less noise. A space for our words to shake out like bird calls and whale songs.

Here is what it all comes down to: In the absence of words is the alone. Not in a way that makes me support constant chatter, but in the way that is curious about how to create connection in this time. And tomorrow. And the many months to come.

Thursday, July 23, 2020

What could be better than a ginger pineapple drink from the café just before the thunderstorm explodes?

Hitting the send button in what looks like a small gesture by the week's end, but it took weeks to get here. Will someone see this work someday and wonder if it was easy? It can look like ease, and grace in the end. Never mind it took soul sweat and heart tears to get there.

But it almost always does.

Even these words are their own kind of practice and some days can have a dose of I Don't Want To But I'll Feel Better If I Do stirred in.

The ginger cutting into the pineapple and balancing the sweet.

Writing projects like today's out of me feel like performing an exorcism on myself. I wish I had another metaphor, but I don't.

I have a part of me that feels haunted and another that feels healed. Neither one owns all the rights.

Today Amelia took a solo journey through her baby book and early childhood albums. She wouldn't share with me but promised we could take another journey through together. Lucy worked their first day as a virtual art camp instructor for their cousins, and they are really so much better with a job, a feeling of their own expertise, a chance to be of service.

Aren't we all.

I'm tired after tonight's send button like someone who's finished a long race and I think I will maybe even relax into sleep like I haven't in some time.

Here comes the thunder now. The lightning and the early darkness.

Here come the watered-down last sips in the cup, a dinner someone else made, and a warm bath after that.

My mind setting down a heavy burden. A complex story puzzle it's been working, but a close-to-the-everything one, too.

It's so strange, I told her today, the way a story can be so past and present at the same time.

Old sorrows and recent ones overlapping. Remnants of a former life I am still dismantling.

Tonight will be all balms and blankets, soft expressions and muscles and thoughts. Yesterday I walked twice and did yoga but not tonight.

Tonight I will be still.

PM

I just wrote one of Anne Carmack's poems into the front of this notebook. It asks, "When was the last time you stayed awake long enough to ache?"

Last night, I want to say. And two nights before that. An ache in my body keeps me awake into wee hours. It's hard to stop craving a body beside me even though I haven't had one for so long. Not just any body. A refuge. A heart home.

Many nights I do not know if I will feel this, or know it, or if it will just be a thing I dreamed of instead of sleeping in those night hours.

I cannot imagine the future. I hardly have a grip on tomorrow. But it feels good to surface a bit, and the weekend does not mean so much. Maybe a nap.

I will sign off early tonight in case sleep might find me, on the tails of these yawns that make my eyes water and burn.

Friday, July 24, 2020

1. Tangled sheets and toenails, the cat launching onto my head all night. A rainy end to the week makes me grateful for yesterday's daring walk to the cemetery before the sky broke loose.

2. The bakery on the way home and the woman running in to ask for help calling 911. She's the manager of a radiology

clinic and she was following a patient who had spit on her employee after being denied entrance for being unmasked.

3. Cops posted up on every other block in my neighborhood and still they can't actually achieve a rapid response. I pass at least one officer on the way home, busy peering in at parked, empty cars.

4. Linus wanting to play, even now.

5. I needed a different song. This one is better, rolling notes and not so heavy.

6. All the recipes I long to make.

7. Wondering what exactly makes a day feel like enough. What makes others feel incomplete or like they slid right through our fingers? What kind of yardstick am I holding up against myself, even in this strange time. It has to be arbitrary and an invention, so why not invent one that makes me feel like a success?

8. Or learn to lay down all the yard sticks and quietly back away.

9. Dreams of a pond (or is it a lake) in Maine. A fireplace. Adirondack chairs on a dock.

10. So many tasks in so many directions, it's hard to know where to start. With the medicine I most need, I think. I want to drop in deep.

11. I want to sleep.

12. I want to watch Miranda July films to fill myself back up.

13. Maybe revisit my card for this month, and perhaps Francisco's words again, for comfort.

14. To let my weighted blanket quiet the jumpiness in my muscles.

15. Find songs for today, for now. Prepare one last farewell and thanks to those I'm stepping back from to make space for something new.
16. But be a little softer with myself. Be kind.

Saturday, July 25, 2020

My tiredness has a distinctive quality in this time, the way pregnancy tired was its own unique sensation. It feels like waking with an ache in my muscles like after a very long walk and craving a hot bath.

But it's morning. And all I've done since last night's bath is sleep. So I linger as long as my morning stomach will allow.

Get up, get up, I whisper to myself.

Feed yourself the good things you've dreamed of all week. Raspberry scones. Sorrel. Risotto. Today is for food. For finding something to listen to while I putter in the kitchen, maybe rolling through some laundry loads while I'm at it.

Last night I left abruptly, while the pizza crust was rising to shake off the day and walk it out on my neighborhood streets. So many Good Evenings and Happy Fridays. Then the park, then the lake with the sun at a 45 degree angle. With reggae music and a woman taking pictures of turtles peeking their heads out above water.

Then a butterfly fell near me, one wing wounded. I pulled out my phone camera to try and capture what was left of her time here.

All I could think as I watched her spin and tumble and drag was:

I feel you.

Soon I waved the photographer over so they could capture it, too.

In the end, it helps to have a witness. To know we don't fall unseen.

The song "exile" - I could listen to Bon Iver forever.

Dear Self, do NOT listen to sad songs all day.

"I think I've seen this film before
and I didn't like the ending"

I'll likely watch *The Squid and The Whale* on Criterion today. So much of the time I try to skate lightly across the surface of life, the way I do in my stories, so I don't have to face the painful parts too directly, or be slowed down or dragged down by them.

But this week my body betrayed me more than once. There are things to feel, and maybe other people's art can help me get there.

I still have Miranda. But so often I'm like someone who needs to eat but can't lift her arms, in a heart way. There is the medicine.

I glance over and think, One of these days I'll get it to my lips. But maybe Noah, first.

"I think I've seen this film before
so I'm leaving out the side door"

Monday, July 27, 2020

Come close. And then a little closer still. Until you can see the new lines in the skin over my heart space and smell the cream I smoothed across my face this morning.

Come close enough to see behind the veil—the feeling behind the presentation. Close enough to hear everything I'm *really* saying when I use the word "fine".

This is what I thirst for, even as one friend posts photos of signs all around the city reminding us to keep apart.

Close is what I miss. Close enough to smell and to reach you, close enough to run gentle hands across the surface of your hair.

I want to step into that place where we leave our need for language next to our shoes by the door and can read everything we need to know as it dances across our faces, syncopated in the pattern of our breaths.

I would pull the air in long at first and billow it out so my cheeks balloon with the expulsion. My eyes would be a song of sadness with a chorus of surrender. The last note would be a light sound of hope, in another key.

I dream of singing out so many songs so new ones might arise in their place.

I want to inhabit a shared space beyond words. Where we set clothing aside and jump into a summer lake in the dark. Where stars overhead can anchor me to the cosmos and time outside my time.

I want to not worry about getting the language right, or all that's flattened in the translation. I just want a natural spring to sit in together. What is there to misunderstand about that?

This is close. A moment wrapping around us like a wide woven blanket. Looking at each other and knowing: We were both here.

This was your life, not your imagination, and there was a witness.

To not have to be in the splendor of aliveness alone, but to know you were alive in it, too.

Maybe we would never speak of it again, or tell another soul, because how could any words hold something so unspeakable?

Maybe you will forget tomorrow, but I won't.

     ✻   ✻   ✻   ✻   ✻   ✻   ✻

I want a coffee table book that is just all the shapes I put my body into during a day. Like now, knee on mattress and elbow leaning. Open. Supported. Tucked in. Turning.

I want a new song that reaches underneath my collarbones. A reminder of a new way to sway or rock. Trying out 5/4 time.

The living could feel like this, the song would teach me, and just as I started to drop into the groove it would break for something completely new from the drums. Here's how to really move, and not just hesitantly. How to move with heels really landing and hip following and arms knowing just where to go. Trumpets would tell them: Here! Now there! Now dropping back to your side and chin following for the gentle landing to the quiet between songs.

To be set carefully back into silence sometimes helps.

What will be the soundtrack of my living today, as even the

coffee doesn't ward off the yawning. What will be my rhythm or beat?

It might just be telling a few people what I'm making, an insurance policy so I don't chicken out. Maybe my body will lay still as my eyes go over so many instructions I wrote to myself.

I will crave an ending like the ones movies give us. They hint that the telling ends here, and so this last moment will be suspended in forever.

But the instructions have no end, even though my Monday morning eyelids crave one.

Neither does the living. The book of stories may end but my heart will beat after the pen rests. The morning will give way to an afternoon and then an evening and a dark night, and tomorrow if I'm lucky the cycle will repeat.

Other words, other days, other times as unimaginable as this one has been.

Other pages, waiting to be filled.

Epilogue • Tuesday, July 28, 2020

The sun is already high above and we are still beginning the day. Sleeping fitfully in the night and catching what other filaments of slumber we can tease from the minutes before noon.

She says she's curious about the part of me that already knows, and that makes two of us.

What do I know, in that deep knowing place? Can I even say it.

I know there is some kind of beauty in me, even if it's hard to pin down or maybe just ever-changing. Something deeper than my daughter saying I have cute feet. (Though I do.)

I have some kind of beauty in me. Also eyes to see uncreated things, and ears to hear unspoken ones. The unplayed notes ring loud at times as if they are calling on me in a class. I know if I refrain and that note finds another it may still come out, but in a way that is not the same. Something is lost and I feel its outline, even as it is clear it will not force itself on anyone.

I know the light and how it shifts and lands and illuminates with its presence and shrouds in its absence.

I know I have ancient agreements inside me and I have been holding back on some level for a very long time.

I know what tenderness feels like and I have been listened to, wordlessly and deeply.

I know listening is an act of love. That the days keep coming and incrementally move us into a new place, even when it feels like we are suspended indefinitely in this here and now.

I know how to hold on and how to let go. How to be mindful

of the stories I tell myself and to try and choose wisely.

That finish lines are overrated and many games were not interesting to play.

I know how to keep breathing through a broken heart. And how loss follows loss like daisies in a chain.

I know I will do what I can today, and every day. But also that my *being* matters, too. Maybe even more.

I know our time here is limited and so much of what I do is an attempt to leave something behind for my kids, and anyone else who needs it.

This is what I know for now.

Thanks and Love • September 14, 2020

I've always loved the work of Laurie Wagner. It is daring in its honesty, and it raises the bar on how high I think courage can go. When she created and shared her *27 Wildest Days* early in the pandemic, it was the time for me and many others to lean into uncertainty with a practice that would both document and anchor us through the turbulent times ahead. I have her, the Wild Writing practice, and her offerings to thank for this collection, which certainly would not otherwise exist. Beyond that, her friendship and long-distance company has been one of this season's most wondrous surprises.

I've tried so many times to learn to catch myself on the page. Always defaulting to some kind of audience, whether blog readers or a friend. It was a relief to finally break through to that field of relationship within and with myself.

This wasn't written for anyone else, or for any other intention or audience, though I started to get the feeling that something about it was taking shape—not currently, as I was writing, but back in the pages behind me. When the final piece came out onto paper I stared at it, thinking, There's the end.

There's no one I'd rather take my generic-looking document and turn it into a work of tangible, hold-it-in-your-hands art than Liz Kalloch, my designer and friend for over a decade. This layout and design are her sublime craftwork. She is a master. A heart of hearts.

Lisa Field sees and hears me in a hundred ways, on a hundred days, but I'm also grateful for the day she saw me through her camera lens and captured these cover and author images. They made me feel more real, more tangible, and not just a wisp of a thought on the wind. Lisa's work brings that kind of gravitas and elevation to all she witnesses.

And much gratitude to Anne Carmack, whose *My Own Body Breathing* is both an inspiration and personal prayer book in these times. It's an honor to include your words at the beginning of this collection (and throughout).

My beloveds are always, always beside me. Across boroughs, miles and oceans. There aren't words that begin to thank them for seeing and loving me, for catching me in sorrow and uncertainty like the safe harbors and shores they are.

I am still emptying good pens, filling notebooks, and showing up with myself on the page most days. My story goes on, and so do I.

About the Author

Jen Lee is the founder and director of Jen Lee Productions, an independent media company based in New York City. She is a celebrated director and producer of three feature-length films: *Gather* (Finalist, Cape Cod International Film Festival 2018), *Bright Lights* (Winner, B Free Awards 2020; World Premiere, Manhattan Film Festival 2017; Official Selection, Adirondack Film Festival 2017) and *Indie Kindred* (World Premiere, World Domination Summit 2013).

Work by EASEL, a division of the company that produces cinema-quality shorts and other promotional materials for creative individuals and organizations, has appeared in the Art Slope Film Festival, *The New Yorker*, and *Vogue*.

On big screens, over radio waves, or in intimate, handwritten pages, Jen's storytelling has a revelatory quality to it, helping viewers and readers experience and understand new or profound concepts and ideas. She also works as a story consultant and coach for a select clientele of activists, innovators, and thought-leaders.

Find more at: www.jenleeproductions.com

CPSIA information can be obtained
at www.ICGtesting.com
Printed in the USA
FSHW020920231120
76093FS